DECODING INDIA'S UNICORN WHICH IS COPIED BY OTHER COUNTRIES

"Deciphering India's Unicorns: a Blueprint for Global Emulation"

SANKALP AWASTHI

BLUEROSE PUBLISHERS
India | U.K.

Copyright © Sankalp Awasthi 2024

All rights reserved by author. No part of this publication may be reproduced, stored in a retrieval system or transmitted in any form or by any means, electronic, mechanical, photocopying, recording or otherwise, without the prior permission of the author. Although every precaution has been taken to verify the accuracy of the information contained herein, the publisher assume no responsibility for any errors or omissions. No liability is assumed for damages that may result from the use of information contained within.

BlueRose Publishers takes no responsibility for any damages, losses, or liabilities that may arise from the use or misuse of the information, products, or services provided in this publication.

For permissions requests or inquiries regarding this publication, please contact:

BLUEROSE PUBLISHERS
www.BlueRoseONE.com
info@bluerosepublishers.com
+91 8882 898 898
+4407342408967

ISBN: 978-93-5989-999-2

Cover design: Tahira
Typesetting: Tanya Raj Upadhyay

First Edition: January 2024

This book is dedicated to my buddy (Dad) and my cute girlfriend (Mom), yaar you both are the greatest supporting pillars. thanks for helping me in every part of life.

In the memory of

Late Mr. Ravi Prakash Awasthi (my bade papa) and my loving Bro Sai Awasthi (my big bro).

IMPORTANT NOTE

Without discipline nobody has achieved anything in his life. Before you begin reading my book, I want one favor from you all. Dude Promise me every day before you go to bed you will read one paragraph from this book. I don't want you to read the whole book right away. I want you to read just one paragraph at a time or a day. That's it, but if you have any excuse or If you belong to the number who just want to finish the book anyhow. then it's my humble request from you please don't read my book, put it down or one more thing you can do return my book. I don't want you to read my book. but if you promise me that you will read one paragraph a day. only then read the next lines.

Dude believe me you are starting a new life with this book. This book can be useless or completely valuable; it's totally up to you to decide.

PREFACE: ACCOMPLISHMENTS

Writing a book is an uncomfortable task because it includes a lot of sacrifices like sleepless nights, not eating on time and a lot of other kinds of pains which can't be told. It's hard to form a good habit, even harder to stick to them. but Being uncomfortable is the only way to grow. I was the guy who always tried to be a multitasker. But trust me bro multitasking is a stupid activity that I was trying to do in life. why I am saying this is the reason there was a time when I was working on my startups, NGO, creating content, doing my research work, giving my interviews, of course writing this book, and so on. I was doing it by myself alone. As a result, I failed to build startups one by one, not being regular in NGO, research was stopped, and this book was on the waiting list.

Which was the lowest point of my life then I went through a worse mental state. Which includes depression, anxiety, and so on. Long story short, every incident in your life gives you a lesson. The lesson I have learned from it is that you can do anything in life but not everything at the same time. So pick one project, give it your best, then move it to another one.

but in the beginning, we see how much we have to do, and it becomes burdensome. take this project (book) for instance. writing more than 1 lakh words? Oh god, I'm feeling excited and a little anxious about it. the guy who doesn't know how to speak fluently using English. Oh man, he is writing his own book by using the same language. hats off to me i am a legend bro but yaar if you found any grammatical error in this book then please forgive me for this mistake I am not as good as you think.

So always enjoy the process of your journey which is more important than the result.

If you are thinking, but Sankalp, enjoying the process is hard. I wanted to achieve my goals, I wanted to be the best version of myself but bro ', then what's the problem dude? Listen if you are desperate about your dreams or goals then you need to accept that there are days that contain self-doubts, distractions, sleepless nights, anxiety, and so on. Whenever you feel any of these things.

I suggest you go for a long drive and try to spend some time with your girlfriend (if she is supportive only then) or with your loved ones And that's completely fine dude.

For some time leaving your goal in a midway is okay. But after refreshing your mood you must have to follow this R, R, R formula (which is Reset, Restart, and Refocus) and restart your work with full passion.

Dude, you have heard this phrase from your dad or anyone, the room wasn't built in a day ? one brick at a time and the same as habit also.

habit will not build in a day. Bro, Now you may understand why I am telling you to read one paragraph at a time or in a day (on an important note) so that you can build the habit of book reading and that's a good habit to include in your life.

If you do, my purpose in writing this book will be successful.

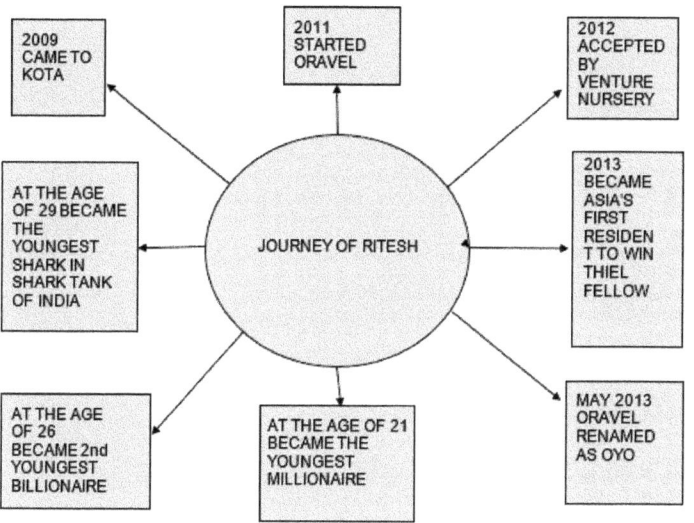

" Don't worry about being successful but work toward being significant and success will naturally follow "

BIO DATA

(:) **NAME** = Ritesh Agrawal

(:) **FOUNDER AND CEO** = Oyo HOTELS AND ROOMS.

(:) **FATHER'S NAME** = Mr Ramesh Agrawal

(:) **MOTHER'S NAME** = Mrs BELA AGARWAL

(:) **BORN** = 16 november 1993 in Bhishma Katek rayagada odisha, india

(:) **AGE** = 30 (till 15 November 2024)

(:) **EDUCATION** = 12th pass And College DropOut.

(:) **MARRIAGE DATE** = 7th march 2023

(:) WIFE = GEETANSHA AGARWAL SOOD

(:) CHILDREN = SON (ARYAN) born on 7th December 2023

(:) NET WORTH = $ 2 billion (as of October 2023)

(:) COMPANY VALUATIONS = $9 billion (till 2023)

TABLE OF CONTENTS

IMPORTANT NOTE v
PREFACE: ACCOMPLISHMENTS vii
INTRODUCTION 1
CHAPTER 1 CHILDHOOD JOURNEY 5
CHAPTER 2 ORAVEL (RISE AND FALL) 24
CHAPTER 3 THIEL FELLOWSHIP 44
CHAPTER 4 INNOVATION BEGIN'S 65
CHAPTER 5 OYO THE UNICORN 96
CHAPTER 6 LOCKDOWN, DOWNFALL AND
BOUNCE BACK 126
CHAPTER 7 ALLEGATIONS AND
CONTROVERSIES 174
CHAPTER 8 SOME UNKNOWN STORIES AND
MINDBLOWING DATA 206
CHAPTER 9   AWARDS AND ACHIEVEMENTS 250
CHAPTER 10 UNCOVERED FACTS AND
INTERVIEWS 255
CHAPTER 11 SPEECHLESS SPEECH 279
BOOKS RECOMMENDATION FROM RITESH 292
RITESH'S ADVICE FOR YOUNG
ENTREPRENEURS 297

INTRODUCTION

"JOURNEY FROM COLLEGE DROPOUT TO THE 2nd YOUNGEST SELF-MADE BILLIONAIRE IN ASIA AND MAKING INTO A UNICORN."

When you think of billionaires, which name comes to mind first? Sir Ratan Tata perhaps ? no doubt he is generally one of the greatest and most successful businessmen.

with 0 haters because of his golden heart (*golden heart ka Mtlb ye nahi hai ki* unka *dil gold ka hai. Mera Mtlb hai ki vo bahut hi* jyada *social work meh involve* rehte *hai). Serious mt lena meri baat majak kr raha tha yaar.So let's come back to the topic. But* most of you think billionaires are aged or to become a billionaire we need a lot of experience or an upper class background in life. dude If you are thinking this then you are on the wrong track with the wrong mindset. bro i suggest you change the way you think. Now you will say yaar kaise karu or how it can be possible bro my friends don't have the same mindset like i have. My family is not supportive. If you have the same excuses of not doing what you wanted to do. so Let me introduce you to the founder and group CEO of Oyo Rooms and Hotels Ritesh Agrawal who was the first asian resident to become a fellow. As impressive as that he was also the second youngest billionaire in the world, 1st youngest billionaire in India, and made into a unicorn. Ritesh has all the stuff we dreamed of. But his journey from rags to riches is not easy for him. Many people used to say that he is lucky but they don't want to see the other side of his journey which includes hard work, dedication, commitment, self-belief, sacrifices, and so on. And I am here to show the other side of his successful startup which we call Oyo. Bro, trust me the story of this guy is very inspiring and motivating for me and I bet that it will definitely inspire and motivate you also. how a small-town boy creates history by making a billion-dollar company at the age of 24 with no high profile and not much financially stable background.

He fits this quote which is that if you have a dream to chase then your age is just a number I know that by reading words like billionaire or self-made billionaire sounds cool but trust me dude for achieving this level of success it takes a lot of hard work, patience, consistency and one of the most important ingredient for success is self beleive. dude remember this every overnight success is at least a few years old painful story.

When Ritesh started his journey of entrepreneurship he faced many challenges. At the age of 17 when he began his journey at that time he was very small.

At the beginning of his journey Whenever he approached hotel owners for partnerships and investors for investments they used to laugh and make fun of him because according to them he was too small for any kind of investments or partnerships. Hotel owners used to think that if I could not make this hotel profitable since I had been running for years then how could this young boy make it profitable? (there is a fact that a 50-year-old man will not believe a guy whose age is 17) and many other people doubted him during his journey But he proved himself in front of everyone by his hard work and self-belief.

Oyo was not the first startup he had started before Oyo. He had tried different businesses which you will come to know when you go through this book thoroughly.

Just think for a while there are many billionaires. Why am I talking about him? What motivated me to write a whole book on him and his company? And let me tell you one more thing: Currently, Oyo is not profitable (according to 2023 data). So if you want to know why / what then read this book you will definitely get the answer to your why / what and if you want to know the reason so for that i have a beautiful answer for you.

"Agar mein abhi sb kuch tumhe bata dunga toh phir tum book mein kya padhoge mujhko. Jara thoda apni aankhon aur hatho ko thoda taklif doo yaar ye Instagram reels ya youtube shorts nhi hai jo ek minute mein sab kuch pata chal jayega jara usse bahar aao aur haa sab kuch baithe baithe nahi milta hai get your shit of reading this book done."

DATA THAT CAN SHAKE YOUR HEAD

- At the age of 20 = he raised money from investors
- At the age of 21 = He hired 50 people
- At the age of 22 = He had 500 hotels
- At the age of 24 = He raised 1 billion dollars
- At the age of 26 = He had 46000 hotels and built the second largest hotel chain in the world
- At the age of 29 = He became the youngest shark on the panel (shark tank India).

So Take a deep breath and tie your seat belt tightly. Let me take you on the journey of a Random guy from an unknown poor city in India who was kicked out of his apartments by his landlord with 35 rupees in his bank account and became the world's youngest billionaire in just 7 years and he, not even 30 (till 2023). from the journey of this guy you will come to know the true meaning of hard work and dedication.

The beginning….

CHAPTER 1
CHILDHOOD JOURNEY

" IF YOU HAVE A DREAM TO CHASE THEN YOUR AGE IS JUST A NUMBER "

Ritesh Agarwal was born into a middle-class family his father used to run a shop of packaging products (like a kirane ki dukaan). but sadly to say that his guiding and supporting star died (on 10 March 2023) due to falling from the 20th floor of a high-rise building in Gurgaon. His mother was a homemaker (housewife). There are 4 brothers and sisters (2 sisters & 1 brother) and he was the youngest among them. As a child, Ritesh had little interest in academics. He preferred to try different things. he was very naughty and curious in his childhood so people used to call him kanha as a nickname (there were many nicknames given to him like natkhat etc but kanha was very popular among them). When his age was between 12 to 13 he heard the word entrepreneur from his elder sister and his elder sister was an inspiration for him or we can say his role model. Then he searched for this word in the dictionary because It sounded cool and unique to him. After that, he said in his mind that yahi banenge but at that period of time he was not generally sure. When Ritesh's sister got a good job in a big IT company then he thought of becoming an engineer. He was also confused like us in different domains for example pilots, lawyers, scientists, engineers, doctors, etc because he used to get inspired by different movies as we do. He always wants to do something different in life. but Like every Indian parent, his parents also dream for their children to be engineers, get a good job, or go to business school and all 4 of them got married. he was a black sheep among his siblings because he always wanted to do something different or wanted to explore different things. Many people used to troll him by saying that kuch nhi karega toh dukaan mein baithega But destiny has some other plan for him.

STARTING HIS CODING JOURNEY

Ritesh's ways were extremely divergent from those of other kids, his fun elements included screwing around with the computer (trying hard to find opportunities to make new mistakes so that he could learn new stuff).

As you know his dad used to run a small business in the city. Whichever company he used to distribute the product For that, it was mandated to have a computer system in which the billing, etc should be done so he bought a 2nd hand computer system for him.

After that all night he uses the computer for doing really random things like, he wrote his first line of code when he was in class 3rd or 4th by using that computer system. For him as a young kid, the first time he saw the stars on the screen a man walked on the screen as an output of that program. He felt for the first time in his life that I could do what I chose to.

As a result, he gained a keen interest in software that started with the idea of knowing more about it, and then hunger just went on. At the age of 8, he discovered his love for coding to know more about software he spent a large portion of his day learning how to code software For that he borrowed his brother's books for programming some of the languages like Basic and Pascal were taught in the school itself and the rest he managed to learn from google mama.

SCHOOL INCIDENT

After listening to the word entrepreneur from his elder sister. When he went to the classroom, the teacher asked every student what they wanted to become (what are their dreams or their future goals). Everyone was sharing their dreams like engineers, doctors, pilots, advocates, some of them wanted to go into the government sector, etc. After listening to the word entrepreneur from his elder sister and looking cool in front of his classmates. He said I will become an entrepreneur but he had no idea what it was or what its meaning was. For him, it was just a different thing. So after that, he kept on saying I wanted to become an entrepreneur.

STARTING HIS OWN BUSINESS

He started his journey by doing random things like selling fmcg products and When he was in class 4 or 5 he started his first business of selling online railway tickets. After that when he was in between class 6 or 7 he moved to his 2nd business of selling sim cards where he was a supporter of a distributor.

Let us understand his businesses in an easy format. where you come to know about many valuable lessons and strategies used by this small and cute boy. Hope you can understand Because I have tried my best to make it simple so that anyone can understand it easily.

ONLINE RAILWAY TICKET BOOKING

Online railway ticket booking was his first business. I know many of you will not believe in this and many of you have been shocked while reading this how such a small boy of class 4 or 5 can do this. Trust me, I was also shocked when I came to know about this.

Let us understand his business model with the help of questions and answers:

Q- Why online?

- As many of you know when online railway ticket booking was not there people used to suffer a lot. They stand in line for 4 or 5 hours for a ticket. When the internet arrived, live inventory began to appear. After that people are ready to give an extra 50 rupees to book their ticket through the Internet.

Q- How does he sell online tickets?

- So he arranged a debit card from someone and a computer (cyber cafe) and he said to local shopkeepers like telephone shops, and grocery stores to take an order of tickets with some cash as an advance. If we can book a ticket we will keep the money but if we can't then we will refund that money till night.

Q- how much profit does he get?

- he gets profit but not that kind of because all those whom he has said to take an order of ticket with some advance they take their share (money) as Ritesh said in his podcast if he books 6 tickets in a day he earns 400 to 500 (rupees) but if ticket gets cancellation fees so he used to pay that amount to satisfy his customer.

GIVING HIS FIRST HARD EARNED MONEY TO HIS MOTHER

When he generated his first income he gave it to his mother. According to Ritesh the money he gave to his mother was 300 or 400 his mother. Before taking money His mother asked if this money was not from doing any wrong thing. So he replied by saying that he earned this money from online railway ticket booking. After hearing this she was very much happy that he earned for the first time on his own. and then she kept it very safely with herself.

SIM CARD SELLING

Sim card selling was his 2nd business and he was a supporter of distributors.

Now the question that will come into the mind of every reader is why / how.

Let us understand his 2nd business model with simple questions and answers. so that we can come to know how such a young boy has used an amazing market strategy to sell his SIM cards.

Q- Why sim cards?

- As we all know Bsnl was only used as a telecom in small cities. but it was changing quickly when private telecom companies or players came. According to Ritesh, airtel was the first private telecom that came to his city (Rayagada). They wanted fine ways of distribution locally. At that point of time, he was very young but he knew a little bit about the local stores there. so here he thought that it was an opportunity to try something new.

Q- strategy/scheme for selling sim cards?

- One of the interviews Ritesh reveals his strategy of selling more sim cards. that he used to take a target by saying he would sell x number of sim cards. Then he started of course devise new ways of making sure that each could sell more sim cards. For example one of the amazing strategies he was started that if you sell 5 sim cards a day then he would host or organize a lunch people in this trade may know there is a scheme that if someone of you sell 5 sim cards then we will host or organize like a lunch for you in a nearby restaurant.

Q- why did he use to provide lunch as an incentive?

- As a class 6 boy he didn't have that much money to spend. So he used to provide lunch as an intensive because the cost of a lunch was very low.

WHEN HE USED TO DO ALL THIS STUFF

Maximum time he did this business was in the summer season. because he used to get lots of time during summer vacation. Worked at 40 to 45-degree temperatures but It didn't matter to him because he had the desire to do this work he did this business till class 10th. He is thankful to His friends who helped him and took him seriously.

DECODING BOTH BUSINESS

After reading his business models and strategies. a simple question arises in your mind how anyone can believe in this small boy for booking railway tickets and a sim card? This same question was asked by Ritesh also and Ritesh replied that the first step is always hard but if the first person gets benefits then everybody else wants to try without bothering about anything. What do you think it is a talent? No dude it is not a talent it is the skill of problem-solving and the ability to create value around yourself and Lots of children have this skill but they don't figure it out or ignore it.

DOES SELLING RAILWAY TICKETS AND SIM CARDS HELPFUL?

Yes By selling railway tickets and SIM cards.helped him to build his unicorn that we know as the name of Oyo. Now the question arises of how these small businesses helped Ritesh to build Oyo. Here are the lessons that Ritesh has learned and applied them when he was building Oyo.

- **customer behavior**
- **small business running people mindset.**
- **Basic economics of business**
- **Oyo boards are inspired by airtel boards**

MAIN LEARNINGS

These 2 lessons have played an important role in his entrepreneurial journey.

- **Don't think any work is small or big. Anything you learn at that time will give you lifetime value and you should take advantage of it.**

- **Always have a hunger to learn something new.**

GOING KOTA

In 2009 he went to Kota Rajasthan for his 11 and 12 education. Why did he go to Kota? While reading the newspaper he saw Kota news many times then he thought that students were doing great there. It will be a good city. He wanted to surround himself with those people who had the same mindset and wanted to try something unique like him. because so much news was coming on Kota. Is Kota his choice? It was absolutely his choice because he was inspired by his elder sister so he partly wanted to pursue engineering as well but he also wanted to be as far away from his home as soon as possible the reason was simple because he wanted to be closer to the cities where new businesses were getting built or something new was happening with the help of the internet. and then he figured out that Rayagada to Kota was a 2 to 3-day journey. so he decided to move to Kota for his further studies. And preparation for the IIT entrance exam. After coming here Apart from studies He loves to explore new and different places with his friends.

REALITY OF KOTA

In all of his childhood he used to feel that the entire Rajasthan used to be only desert and sand dunes. After landing in Rajasthan he realized that there were roads and rivers there. The interesting story of Kota is that whatever happens in Kota the only excuse is Chambal water (chambal ka paani). if food was very spicy people would say this due to chambal water (chambal ke pani ke karan hai) people would hate you and in the outdoors, people would scream at you whenever you want to negotiate something. (like yeh gussa bhi chambal ke pani ke karan aata hai).

Soon he came to know what people were doing around him was something different from what I wanted to do. He enjoyed all of his childhood through the different 10th grade. He felt that so many engineers are coming out from Kota so everyone should be doing something really cool.

In a month and a half, he realized that almost everyone was either mugging up what was in organic chemistry or was doing something that would help them solve problems and get to the next examination. he thinks that he never really connected with that.

INTERNSHIP JOURNEY

Have you heard this line kooye ka mendak (frog) or the less you explore the less you know about the world? The same line follows on Ritesh. when he was in Rayagada he was very happy because he didn't know about any other cities. But when he came to kota for the first time he was shocked by seeing that students were coming from the whole of India like Uttar pradesh, madhya pradesh, Rajasthan, Delhi, Mumbai, and many other places. he got a lot of amazing opportunities to learn from them but he always wanted to do something unique as he has done with train tickets booking (booking tickets online) and selling airtel sim cards.

So a year and a half after that he used to take a weekend train from Kota to Delhi and started working for free for startups. (means to do small internships) he used to do coding, selling products and making social media pages. (for that point of time by making a facebook page you could charge a small amount). And all sorts of things he felt it was amazing to learn from things like this.

Does he know coding? According to him at that time he knows languages just like HTML. and HTML is not a language. Now one more question comes to your mind: why I have not named the coding languages that Ritesh knows because Ritesh has an allegation that he doesn't know any languages at all. I have covered all this controversy in the next part of this book volume 2.

KOTA TO DELHI AND MUMBAI

He loves to read books and biographies of successful businesses and startups.

He used to take weekend trains to Delhi (and Mumbai) and attend all of these startup events because it was the first time when entrepreneurship was getting started (and there he met some extremely smart people). from Kota to Delhi it takes 3.5 hours of time. Sometimes he used to come with his bunch of other friends because they wanted to spend time partying and so on.He didn't have that much money to do it and he cannot sneak into places like those. but he can sneak into startup events/startup conferences because when he goes to startup conferences it is very difficult for him to pay the money like $100 (registration cost) to attend the startup conferences. This means he didn't have that much money to pay for every startup event/startup conference that he wanted to attend. but other side he felt that this was the right place for him. So he realizes something amazing very early in his life. There are 2 kinds of people who attend startup events / startup conferences.

1) People who have money (like good and smart people). means who pay the price of the event (registration cost) and get's the card (startup event card / event id card) and then access conferences.

2) People who don't wear anything like cards (startup event card/event ID card) are more / most important people at the conferences/events.

So he told himself that if i have to get into these events / conferences the best way is not to wear this card (startup event card/event id card) and to say that I am the more / most important guy. So he sneaked into these events because he could not afford the registration cost or buy cards for every event that he wanted to attend. So He used to try to go to these events without the card. Many allowed him because he was too Small. According to him when he was attending the entrepreneurial events he saw Kunal then just came back from the US and wanted to start entrepreneurial ventures. And many more entrepreneurs, startup founders, and so on. First time he realizes that entrepreneurship should be broader. When he attended a very big event in Delhi that was a **tie event (the Indus Valley entrepreneur).** and that is One of the events that changed his life.

At 16 Ritesh was selected among the 240 children to be part of the Asian Science Camp held at the Tata Institute of Fundamental Research (TIFR) in Mumbai. The camp is an annual forum for pre-collegiate students, aimed at promoting discussion for the betterment of science in the region.

WRITING BOOK

As you all know he loves to travel and explore new or different places while traveling in Kota he came to know about many engineering colleges. He did something that no other student had done.

So during his free time on his hand he started writing a book which was a huge success on Flipkart and sold in large numbers and also contributed to Ritesh Agarwal success story (according to some websites at that time his age was 17).

Book name: " Indian Engineering colleges A Complete Encyclopedia of top 100 Engineering Colleges".

Published: 2011

Published by (publisher): G.K Publisher.

Written by (author): Ritesh Agarwal

FIRST TURNING POINT

His first turning point was in 2010. when he joined the startup event named tie event in Siri fort auditorium (the Indus entrepreneur). the first time he saw extremely smart people who had conventional and unconventional impact items that they wanted to do in their lives. According to him, he got an opportunity to meet and talk to various vcc's, ceo's, investors, and angel investor startup founders like Sanjeev Bikhchandani (who is Sanjeev Bikhchandani? Sanjeev Bikhchandani is an Indian businessman, who is the founder and executive vice chairman of Info Edge which owns Naukri.com, a job portal, as well as the co-founder of Ashoka University. He was honored with the Padma Shri, India's fourth highest civilian award, in January 2020) and so on. He saw Kunal then just came back from the US and wanted to start entrepreneurial ventures. he was so curious to talk and to know about them he went inside the event without any id card (startup event card/event id card) and at that time he was between 16 or 17. One thing that he found amazing about people in startups was people were so accessible that you could walk up and talk to them. Means Overall he saw and met all these people who were extremely smart in their particular field. After meeting them soon he realized 2 things.

1) He wanted to surround himself with smart people like these and do whatever is required.
2) He will build a company at some point of time but he still kept it internally (in his mind).

After completing his class 12th. He had a gap of 6 months before he joined any college and in that certain period of time he was dive enough to think that he should start a company on his own.

QUITTING KOTA

Ritesh soon came to know that he could not make it into IIt or he realized that this culture was not meant for him so he quit Kota and moved to Delhi in 2011. To start up something of his own and also to prepare for the SAT to go to the US for further studies. He doesn't have money-related problems because he had savings from Kota and the pocket money was good (roughly 15000 for a month). Fortunately or unfortunately the SAT never happened and after 1 year of meeting people, reading about startups, and traveling he came to know about the gaps between customers and hotel owners he came up with the idea of Oravel which is similar to Airbnb.

BECOMING THE YOUNGEST CEO OF INDIA

When he was 17, he became the youngest chief executive officer (CEO) in India. Of a company called Worth Growth Partners. Let me explain his startup by question and answer which was asked by the interviewers (this interview was done on Thursday, May 19, 2011, which is covered by your story).

Q- What does worth growth partner startup do?

- They are primarily a service company providing almost all the solutions a foreign company needs in India. As their name worth growth partners signifies they are the partners of our growth. This means they provide consultation to foreign companies that are entering Indian markets (consultation companies).

Q- How did the idea of this startup come from his mind?

- One day Ritesh was in conversation with his entrepreneur friend from Germany. He described to him how difficult it was for other German and foreign businesses to establish and develop in India. After that Ritesh personally started researching about it and got in touch with his friends from Miami, Singapore, and Delhi who were prospective team members for the same. Luckily he was appreciated when they heard that he was talking about developing a one-stop service platform for foreign business to develop in India. Furthermore, this idea was nurtured by adding the service range for Indian companies.

Q- where are Worth growth partners located ?

- Worth growth partners' headquarters are located at G-82 Greater Kailash, Greater Kailash Nct, 110048, India.

Q- what is your revenue model?

- As our name, worth growth partners signifies, we are partners of your growth and progress. We partner you, get the project executed and ask for a simple payment for the same.Our business relies on the strategy that good work is noticed. So, we primarily concentrate on providing the best services. I primarily re-invested the money that I had gained from my previous startup and consulting projects along with some investments from bank overdrafts.

Q - why do they believe you ?

- Although we are into a business which could be termed as innovative, I would not say we sit on the edge without any competitors. I have been an entrepreneur, technology executive, social marketer, sales executive and even a salesman.and Personally, I am regarded as the world's youngest CEO by various agencies, since I started when I was 13 and am really young even now. I have also authored a best seller book.

We have a number of tie ups but since some of them are internal and some of them are under process to reach the pen and paper stage so it wouldn't be easy for me to give their names. But I can say all of them are best in their fields in the Indian industry and many of them in the global industry too.Yeah, we have a tremendous acceptance of the concept.

Overall I can acclaim with humility that I have that in me to understand and customize any business for the Indian consumer because I understand them. I also have a pretty good sense of understanding the foreigners which primarily gives us a breakthrough in better communication strategies.We are on our way to growth mutually and that's what makes us say worth growth partners are your partners in growth all the way.

Q- As an entrepreneur, what are your joys? What are the challenges?

- I wouldn't say that the best joy is about not having a boss because being an entrepreneur you have multiple bosses including your customer, legal executive, ca etc. The joy is leading a team, doing something of your own, taking risks, bringing out something out of nowhere. And, the most important one(on a funnier note), you earn lots of bucks (money).

CONFUSION

He had 2 options very early in life. He had started doing a bunch of research he was doing on urea which is how urea combined with water becomes ammonia which is not great. On the other side, he was doing entrepreneurial ventures and during this entire period he was unable to make a decision on what side to go to. Then he found amazingly a wise man whom later on he had gifted some shares of his company (oyo) to make sure that he had thanked him for this huge benefit. This man asked him a very interesting question.

Man said : Beta atom chahiye ya itum.

Ritesh replied : Why are you asking this?

Man said : Ritesh there are 2 kinds of people.

1) **who dedicated their lives towards creating something that changes a world a few generations later.**
2) **The people who are really hungry to see an impact.**

Ritesh replies: I am the guy who wants to see that impact and I want to work really hard then I wanna see the impact immediately which is what he said hence the item makes a lot of sense so from that day onwards Ritesh had never researched or opened any of his research books and his entrepreneurship began.

WHAT YOU HAVE LEARNT NOW, MAKE SOME NOTES SO THAT YOU CANNOT FORGET

CHAPTER 2
ORAVEL (RISE AND FALL)

" LIFE PRESENTS YOU WITH 2 OPPORTUNITIES OR 2 OPTIONS AT ALL CERTAIN POINTS OF TIME. EITHER TAKE A RISK OR REGRET.TAKING RISK IS BETTER THAN REGRETTING IN LIFE "

WANTED TO START ORAVEL AS AN INDIAN Airbnb

Before starting Oravel. He felt that most Indian successful companies have some or other emulation of an American company. He thought if he used half of his brain to do the same thing. then he would also become successful. because He saw that Airbnb was successful. So he said I would be the Airbnb of India (which means he launched Oravel Stays Pvt. Ltd by inspiration of Airbnb) So that's how he had started Oravel to begin with.

ORAVEL

In 2012 he started his first company. that is Oravel Stays Pvt. Ltd. Oravel was the first brand he started. which was India's first platform for listing and booking low-cost lodging (कम लागत वाले आवास की बुकिंग).

- Villas
- Services apartments

- Bed and breakfast
- Small hotels

All these unknown places are listed on a website with their prices.

WHY ORAVEL AS A DOMAIN NAME

Because Oravel was only left as a domain name for travel and other domain names are full. (Oravel means outside travel) and one more thing this domain name was cheapest. Their mindset for taking domain names was simple. It should be cheap and contain travel because by him the company / brand name is not very important.

The things that are important to him are Your services, customer reviews, affordable prices, and good locations.

COMMENT ON DOMAIN NAME

For starting any startup domain names does not matter as you see google it is not cool but because of its popularity people appreciate it same as amazon, Microsoft, etc but for many people domain name matters a lot for example you know Anupam mittal (founder of shaadi.com) he had raised $ 30000 for the company shaadi.com but here is a twist guess how much he had paid for his domain name let me reveal it $ 25000. see the craziness for domain name. Elon Musk paid $ 75000 to Brad Siewert in 2004 to buy Tesla as a domain name. Every founder has their own opinion or you say their own point of view for taking domain name for their company..some focus on their brand, some on their name, some on their service, and some focus on uniqueness. however everyone is right I am not saying wrong to anyone each and everyone is trying their best to grow their companies but if you ask From my point of view I am totally satisfied with Ritesh because. Why do we have to waste so much money on domains or luxurious things? In fact, we can utilize that money to improve our customer services because your customer repetition does not depend on your cool domain name. They will come again again because of your good quality of services. your affordability of product or does your product create value in their life. and one more thing how you make them feel (aura) because every human being has an emotional side. and these all things are greater than any stylish or cool domain name for me. because you give a domain name to your startup so that people may know about your startup. domain name plays a 20 % to 30 % role in your startup. Your startup is not run by domain name it runs by your customer.

RISING OF ORAVEL

when he was in class 11 and 12 he used to get a stipend by doing small internships like making social media pages, websites, and so on. He loves to travel and explore new places so he travels alone or sometimes with his intern every weekend he takes a bus from Anand Volvo bus from Vihar ISBT and goes where a bus can take him to places like Rajasthan, Uttarakhand, Himachal pradesh jammu and kashmir, etc.and spend a weekend on those places.

By traveling in different cities he noticed 2 huge problems.

Problem 1

Those places are very expensive to stay in. and his budget for pocket money was very limited.

So every weekend he used to write an email to the hotel owners asking to let me stay for free (which means asking for a free room). I will solve something in this sector someday. because he has a huge hunger for solving problems in this sector. Some let him stay free, some give discounts, but many of them say you have to pay the whole price.

Problem 2

When he was traveling from one place to another in search of budget-friendly rooms. So he used to read travelers' blogs for accommodation (awas, house) which helped him to connect with local landowners and so on. After that, he came to know that there are a large number of unknown places like small guest houses, holiday homes, hotels, etc which are generally undiscovered by the people. They provide average places with the right price.(which means budget-friendly places).

But they are not available on the internet or any kind of platform and also not discovered by many people or travelers and these property owners are almost saying we should sell it because there is no need at the end of every month.

So he felt that there is a large number of problems that should be solved by both the consumer side and the owner side. And then he thought I would make an online travel agency for offbeat locations (offbeat = not discovered by the people). where we list all the unknown and undiscovered places on a website. That's why he launched Oravel or you can say the rise of Oravel. Oravel is very similar to Airbnb India where they connect travelers to hotels, service apartments, and so on.

WORKING ON ORAVEL

He started making a list of all the unknown places with the help of interns. I know now the question comes to your mind: who are his interns and how did he come to know about them ? with the help of internshala. He finds them and they help him by providing the list of unknown places or by coordinating them by phone. So he created a list of unknown places and distributed them into a website with their price. While building Oravel 2 things were happening.

1) He let's consumers book accommodation online (awas, room)
2) He continues traveling and staying at new bed and breakfast hotels. For that, he had escaped the emails of hotel owners and asked them to stay with him for free. some let him to stay but many won't.

He tried to run his business (Oravel) in between 6 months to 12 months (1 year). But there was no booking or a small amount of booking and the repeat rate was also very low.

TRYING TO BUILD ORAVEL

When he was working on Oravel he saw some light of success. but it was not, it was just the start of his failure or you can say his struggle came up.

All the savings he had spent in staying in 100 places in India in more than 200 properties (hotels, bed & breakfast, service apartments, and so on).

Over these 6 to 12 months periods of time. It sounds like a less number considering 365 days a year (1year).

At that point of time, a lot of people had said to him you have gone mad or what. You have a little bit of savings and You live away from your home/family which is in Odisha.you're spending all your money on holidaying and staying in hotels in the northern half of India.

Because he was staying in so many properties.he was broke (no money).

STRUGGLING TIME CAME UP

When he was broke he had 2 options at that point of time.

1) Either go back to college
2) Or call his family and they will call him back.

When he ran out of money in his pocket (broke) at night, he called his family because he had less money but he couldn't speak because if he spoke anything, his family told him to take the train, (son) and come back. After that He asked his friends for money but His friends mostly are all college students but they usually had the same pocket money that he had. So he had to sleep on the stairs for 12 days on the same property where he was actually staying because his landlord wouldn't let him in before he paid his dues (flat rent) or cleared his dues (flat rent).

His family was financially good. It is not that his family could not help him during that bad phase / bad time he had.

But the problem is if he picks up the phone and being an 18 year old child tell's his family that he has no money (broke) the first thing they will say is to come back home.

in one of the speeches, he said that as an entrepreneur you would know when you really want to create something it is the last thing you have to do is basically stop midway and go back.

Because he had a huge hunger for problem solving. And he desperately wanted to give his best and he knew that he had not given it all.

CAME TO KNOW THE REAL PROBLEM

At the same time He heard from consumers who were staying with him as well as himself,one of the people who was also traveling. he realized that the discovery of an accommodation was a very small problem already. We can find many hotels, guest houses online. The problem was in predictability.

PREDICTABLE EXPERIENCE

It is the overall satisfaction of a hotel's guests before, during, and after their stay. It's the interactions a hotel has with its guests from before they check-in to after they leave.

If you want to make it clear read the next paragraph that is REALITY BEHIND HIS FAILURE.

REALITY BEHIND HIS FAILURE

When He fails continuously in building Oravel.The reality behind his continuous failure was everyone who stayed with them came back with their issues/reviews which were significantly different.

- We landed in the city and called the hotel owner. He didn't pick up the phone.
- We reached the hotel but couldn't get in because it was locked.
- Problem on reaching the hotel because of no sign board.

- Reach inside the hotel receptionist is sleeping topless.
- Room is smelling badly
- Bedsheets are torn apart.
- Tv is not working.
- Quality of a room is very poor
- Switches / sockets are not working
- Washroom don't have water
- Leakage all the time
- Credit is not acceptable
- Breakfast has worms / is unhygienic

There were all sorts of issues like these and It used to be a ridiculous experience.

Then he came to know that booking can be done but no one is taking the responsibility of service quality. He felt terrible about it and decided to solve this problem of predictability.

HOW HE WILL FIX PREDICTABILITY

He said that he wanted to fix predictability and globally this was never done. Nobody who was a tech brand went out and said we would fix predictability in a space that has a very very low occupancy rate. because there are moments of failure. it is not like a cab (ola, uber)the point of arrival is a failure. Here point failures are more than 100 all the way from check in to check out.

all the way from when customers check in to check out of the hotel.

He had to see that

- The television is in working condition
- The socket is working
- water is available in the washroom
- The bedsheet is not torn apart
- The room is not smelling badly
- Breakfast should be hygienic
- Credit Card should be accepted

And so on……..

DON'T WANT TO START NEW BUSINESS

As a child Ritesh had a hunger to solve problems or he wanted to create an impact.

So at the age of 19 one thing became very clear to him after knowing the problem of predictability in hotels, Appartements and so on. He did not want to build anything which meant one more business.(he thought of starting one more online business while building oravel) because he really wanted to do something that created a real impact. If he fails, he will learn a lot. And if he wanted to create a business would have done it anyway through his life.

DOUBTERS

When he came to know about this problem (problem of predictability). He started approaching a lot of people whom he knew at that point of time or you can say that He started talking to a lot of people and he said I wanted to solve this problem. This is a real problem out there which is having predictable experiences in these hotels. Why don't I solve it? A lot of people used to tell him that look what you were doing, the online thing was a cooler one now you want to go to start a hotel this is a boring thing no one will fund ideas like this. he said i am not building this get funding i am building this because i feel that there is a large problem and people felt that this guy was just ridiculing everyone around because everyone does startup to raise funding overall everyone told him this is not scalable.

At that point of time he was doing a lot of reading. He heard something amazing which he felt very deeply about. and he did a lot of reading time. Steve Jobs once said " **INNOVATION IS WHAT DIFFERENTIATE LEADER VS FOLLOWERS "** He said I don't want to be a leader, I want to be someone who creates and solves something. and does not do something for a business.

DECIDED TO FIX PREDICTABILITY

When he came to know about predictability he decided that he would fix it. If it means that he would not build something that 1000 people kind of like. he will build something that 5 people will fall in love with. which means if he operates only 1,2 hotels he will operate them so well that customers would have a better experience than today. may not be 5-star type or may not be foolproof but definitely way better than today and they can predict what kind of experiences they gonna get. During the same time came with turning periods of his life.

GOING TO COLLEGE

Right after his 12th he told his parents that he would go to college. so He enrolled in a college which was University of London's India campus in Delhi. He went there for 2 to 3 days after that. He was postponing the next day because he felt that he would go for the next day. One day he took a leave and stayed back to continue building oravel which was slowly becoming more predictable.So he kept postponing that 1 day 1 day kept pushing into 6 months.

His family did not even know that in the place of going to college, he stayed back there and building this company (oravel).

FIRST FUNDIND

As we all know that At the age of 18 (in 2012), he founded Oravel Stays,a budget - friendly hotel accommodation portal This start-up was accepted into the accelerator program by Venture Nursery after that He got in touch with accelerator Venture Nursery, flew down to Mumbai and got seed funding of around Rs 30 lakh.

Q - what is seed funding ?

'Seed funding' is the funding for a startup when it is at the seedling stage i.e., inception, ideation, or the beginning stage. It is essential for every entrepreneur to understand what constitutes seed funding and why it is essential for building their businesses.

Venture nursery

- It was established in March 2012.
- It was India's first angel-backed startup accelerator program it is located in Mumbai
- The company's model is top support startups and entrepreneurs in their early stages
- It runs a 13 weeks acceleration program during the program startups work with angels - in - residence and charter angels to improve their business proposition and team
- Venture nursery conduct twice or thrice boot camps a year
- Venture nursery selects up to 12 startups teams or individuals twice a year the selected startup receive financial support in the form of :

  (i) pre - seed funding

  (ii) work space

  (iii) it facilities

  (iv) other resources
- Venture nursery was the first investor in oyo rooms; it held around 2% stakes in the company and exited with Rs 60 crore in a secondary sale of shares.
- VentureNursery undertakes intensive and immersive coaching and mentoring roles in the chosen startups and helps each with end-to-end infrastructural and learning support. With an obsessive focus on quality, VentureNursery, currently, conducts two to three boot camps a year in Mumbai and accommodates two startups in each for a three-month period. It also runs a separate program called ParallelTrack whose duration may vary between ten and forty weeks. Both programs

involve heavy customization based on the startup's requirements.

Founders of venture nursery

- **Shravan shroff :** founder and former md of fame india limited (fame cinema)
- **Ravi kiran :** former ceo of south east & south asia for starcom media vest group and co - founder of friends of ambition

Shroff and Kiran both came from business families. Shroff's family was in movie distribution and kiran's family was in jewelry. Neither joined the family buissness.

Shravan shroff

Ravi kiran

successful Startup came from venture nursery

Venture nursery has accelerated 21 startups of which 16 have graduated. 12 of those startups are active and growing well.

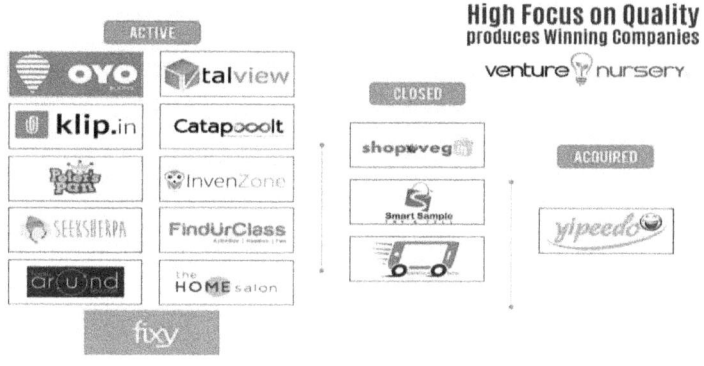

And so on

CONVINCING PARENTS FOR DROPPING COLLEGE

After class 12 when he thought about starting his company, he had an open conversation with his parents. He called them and had an open conversation about his business. Of course, they were disappointed when they came to know that he was planning something else in the place of going to college(pursuing engineering). Because he comes from a small town where if you have to leave this little town or want to do anything better in life. For them, life is better when you get a good job with a middle class income lifestyle. The only way to do it is to get a college degree.(this means his parents wanted him to complete his college, get a degree and get a decent job)that is what his parents knew.

when he called his father for the first time and said "I want to become an entrepreneur." At the same time, some people came to know about his thiel fellowship program.his father has supported him very much (means he became his supporting pillar) and said if you want to pursue entrepreneurship you can. However, he convinces his father (partly).

But his mother was disappointed by his decision of not going to college or dropping out. because as an Indian typical parent she wanted that his son to go to college (university) and get a good job.

His mother used to say that if you don't get the degree, who will marry you (because in arranged marriages they want to see the biodata of the person). And if you don't write your college degree in your biodata then how will you get married? He convinced his mother by saying give me 1 or 2 years. Within that period of time I want to build my company. If I can't then I will go back to college. He doesn't want to go to college again. but to convince her mother He and his father have made a plan that he will say all this to his mother. and their plan was successfully executed because after that his mother agreed (she was convinced).

He also told his mother and father that many people take a year gap after 12th.

Aap maan lijiye ye mera year gap hai agar kuch acha nhi kr pata toh wapas chala jaunga college aur waise bhi college konsa bhaag raha hai.

It takes 2 to 3 days to convince his parents.

DOES DROPPING OUT IS THE RIGHT DECISION ?

This question was asked by Ritesh in one of the interviews and he answered this question with simple and understandable language.

He said: No doubt education is very important, education is very critical. I believe in it wholeheartedly but when I signed the agreement for this fellowship (theil fellowship) the first line was we never let university interfere with education

So education can be anywhere. I was getting by being on the field somebody will get an education by being in their own respective segment or field of interest but really what matters is are you pursuing education or not. College or university is a great way to access it but there are many other ways of getting an education.

When I was building my business at that point of time I didn't know what it meant to drop out of college (university). I love doing it so I am pursuing it anyhow. Now when I look back I feel it was such a bad idea because after that I had no other choice if oyo did not turn out I would basically be the no graduate (no college degree holder) and no business.

I probably feel like naivety (bholapan) is very critical (gambhir) when you are building your business.

But getting the right kind of education is also very much important in life.

COMMENT:

Maybe you cannot understand the above answer which was given by Ritesh so i tried my best to explain it in my language where i have tried my best to elaborate it as much as I can so that you can understand it in an easy way.

I hope you can understand it.

If I ask you what is the source of education? or from where we get it?

your answer will be to get the education we must have to go to school or college. No doubt education is very important in our life. According to my point of view, we must pursue full education when we are in school because at that point of time, we don't know what to do in life or what our goal is and that we are confused and naive enough to do anything. But after completing school we get enough time between school and college that period of time we can try what we want to or where we can give our best. It can be anything so that we cannot regret it that we have not tried it. For example, I can be an actor but I have not tried it at all or I have not given my best in this field. I know now you will ask if we will not go to college, how we will pursue education, or how we will get education. (Here is a twist) Everybody has different methods of taking education or gaining any kind of knowledge. Education is everywhere but how we grab it is totally our point of view. For example : someone gets an education by working on the ground like Elon musk, steve jobs and there are many examples like them.

Overall my suggestion is if you want to do something in life just go through it. take your first step towards it.

Here I have answered some questions that are coming to your mind and making you confused after reading all this stuff.

Q- when to take a drop out and what things you must know when you are dropping out.

When to take a drop out ?

- Education is very important in life but going to college or any kind of university is not only the source of getting education, many people get education by working in the field, and many people get it by doing self education. We have the best examples of Steve jobs, bill gates, walt disney, Mukesh ambani, gautam adani and many others. who does not go to any college or dropped out of college and created a billion dollar company. But I am not saying that if you don't want to study just drop out of college. It is not a joke or not it sounds like cool stuff to do. It is a very hard decision which you are taking in your life because this decision can make you or destroy you. on which basis you will drop out.. They have dropped out because they want to chase their dream which is bigger than any kind of degree. and they all believe in practical knowledge or you can say that knowledge that came from working in the field.If you want to drop out you must have clarity in your dream. I am not saying that if you want to open a startup/business. Then only you can drop out.Your dream can be anything (but see that you must have good intentions or add some values to others life not harm someone intentionally or physically). you just have to make it clear by small execution. when you work on your dream you will get clear that it is your true calling/dream or its just kind of attraction. because there is a thin line between attraction and dream and it will clear only when you put daily small effort on it.

Things you must know when you are dropping out.

2 things you must know when you are dropping out of college.

1) You must know any kind of skill, knowledge or you have any talent.
2) You have a dream to chase. for you which is bigger than any kind of degree.

If you come under any of the above points then you can drop out from your college.

WHAT YOU HAVE LEARNT NOW, MAKE SOME NOTES SO THAT YOU CANNOT FORGET

CHAPTER 3
THIEL FELLOWSHIP

> " IF SOMEBODY OFFERS YOU AN AMAZING OPPORTUNITY BUT YOU ARE NOT SURE YOU CAN DO IT, SAY YES THEN LEARN HOW TO DO IT LATER! "

Before continuing the journey of Ritesh I want to let you know about this beautiful opportunity. which has helped Ritesh a lot with exposures, funding, and so on. which is thiel fellowship lets us decode this and know everything about it.

THIEL FELLOWSHIP

Thiel fellowship was started by Peter Thiel who was the one of founders of Paypal. and one of the earliest investors in facebook.(He also was Facebook's first big investor, and has sold off most of his stake, turning his initial $500,000 investment into more than $1 billion in cash) If you have seen a social network movie you see the guy who first hands over the check to facebook founder (mark zuckerberg).

This guy is Peter Thiel

Paypal

Paypal is an online payment processor platform. where we can receive and send money / payment in the world. We can call it a third party payment gateway method.

What is thiel fellowship

Candidates with a creative bent of mind may apply for the Thiel Fellowship. The fellowship was founded in 2011 by Peter Thiel, a technology entrepreneur and investor. The Thiel Fellowship Scholarship has a grant amount of

$100,000 and covers a two-year program. The fellowship is open to young people who are 22 years or younger with a penchant for building new things. A key feature of the scholarship is the award recipient has to skip or stop out of college to receive the fellowship.

Thiel Fellowship At a Glance

1. The Peter thiel Scholarship is granted to around 20-30 individuals every year.
2. Thiel fellowship acceptance rate is 0.1% indicating that it is highly competitive.
3. The fellowship is not limited to software engineers, as some assume it to be. In fact, it is open to any "young people who want to bring their ideas to the world."
4. The application form for Thiel Fellowship 2023 is open year-round. So one may apply whenever they feel like it.
5. To accept the Thiel fellowship scholarship, the recipient has to drop out. This holds true even for school-goers.
6. Also, Thiel Fellowship winners 2023 don't have to move to San Francisco, as Thiel Fellows are based all over the world.

Thiel Fellowship Eligibility Criteria

One of the primary criteria is the Thiel fellowship age limit that is 22 or younger for applicants. For students who are in school, Thiel fellowship requirements mandate dropping out their studies to pursue their ideas. In addition, there are other thiel fellowship eligibility criteria that the fellowships grant committee will decide based on applications submitted by applicants. Also, considering the fellowship is meant for young people who want to build new things, the applicant must be able to showcase that he/she has bright ideas as thiel fellowship acceptance rate is extremely low at 0.1%. Those who fulfill the thiel fellowship eligibility criteria can apply throughout the year, at any time of the day.

How to apply for thiel fellowship

The application form for Peter Thiel Fellowship is open in online mode and can be submitted by candidates who meet prescribed eligibility criteria of Thiel Scholarship. Considering the Thiel Fellowship application form is open 24/7, one can apply anytime one wants.

Steps to fill application form for Thiel Fellowship

Step 1 - Thiel Fellow application registration

To register, follow the steps listed below.

1. Go to the registration portal of Peter Thiel scholarship.
2. Click on the Sign Up option.
3. Enter valid email id and password. Confirm password.
4. On correctly entering the required details, a candidate account will be created.

Step 2- Profile creation

The candidate has to next create a profile by entering details like name, email id, and date of birth.

Step 3 - Thiel Fellowship Application form filling

To start the thiel fellowship application process, click on the Edit button, upon which a detailed application form will open up. Give an email ID that is actively in use to fill the Thiel fellowship application.

1. First name
2. Last name
3. Email address
4. Date of birth
5. Hometown
6. Current Location
7. Current work address and location
8. Project/company link
9. Linked link
10. What cool stuff have candidates worked on in the past?
11. Are candidates open to co-founding a startup with a different idea?
12. Are they currently attending college?
13. Do they currently have any eligible co-founders (22 and younger and without a college degree)?
14. Would you like to recommend someone (22 or younger and without a college degree) for the Thiel Fellowship Scholarship?
15. How did candidates hear about the Thiel Fellowship Scholarship?

The candidate has to submit completed application forms.

Some question was asked regarding thiel fellowship

1. What is the Thiel Fellowship?

The Thiel Fellowship is meant for young entrepreneurial people who want to create something new. The fellowship is for two-year and is worth a $100,000 grant.

2. When will registration open for Thiel Fellowship and what is the deadline?

Applications are received and reviewed year round, so you can apply any time you want. Also, updates in applications are allowed even after submissions.

3. Tell me something unique about the fellowship?

To accept the Thiel Fellowship, you need to drop out.

4. What is the age limit to apply for Thiel Fellowship?

The applicant needs to be aged 22 or younger to apply.

5. Is the Thiel Fellowship worth it?

People who have been awarded the Thiel Fellowship say that it was totally worth it for them.

6. How long does it take to hear back from the Thiel Fellowship?

It takes about a month or so after your application from the Thiel Fellowship whether they would go ahead with your application or not.

7. How many Indians won the Thiel Fellowship?

Two Indians have won the Thiel Fellowship until now.

8. What is the acceptance rate for the Thiel Fellowship?

The Thiel Fellowship is highly competitive and its acceptance rate is merely 0.1%.

9. How do you qualify for the Thiel Fellowship?

Your application will be reviewed by the Thiel Foundation members. If they find your work innovative enough, your application will be selected. After this, you will be required to drop out of school and focus on works like scientific research, a startup creation, or work on a social movement.

Now come back to the story ....

APPLYING AND BECOMING AN INDIA'S FIRST THIEL FELLOWS

2013 is when ritesh agarwal became a thiel fellow. but the story of applying to become a fellow is quite funny and was very much interesting.vo kehte hain naa agar kisi cheez ko dil se chaho toh puri kainaat usse tumse milane ki koshish mein lag jaati hain.This quote fits in his story of applying for thiel fellowship.

When he was searching for Peter Thiel in the cyber cafe,(why did he go to the cyber cafe ? He goes to a nearby cyber cafe because he did have internet access at the place he was living in at that point of time so he had to go to a nearby cyber cafe where people could use the internet and so on) he found a Thiel website then he reached out to some of his friends and they have heard about it as well.and one of his friend Apurv mishra who is from odisha recommended him to apply. So randomly he applied.

Here comes an interesting part of this story.the last date of applying is 12 o'clock at night. He felt that it was game over. I have never been able to make up for filling the document (form) interestingly (he was frustrated at that point of time). He woke up the next morning. he was like oh god how did i crash out and turns out time zone helps help him to make sure that he still get few hours to fill the form(because the reality is pacific standard time vs indian standard time which helps him) so he just got in at the last moment.

He never knew that he would actually make it because before him there was no other Indians or Asian resident who had become a fellow (thiel fellow) so he thought there was no chance I would become a fellow. but still he applied (hamara toh hone nahi hai).

Because the application process was very much interesting for him.

While applying he was surprised and happy by reading that he would get paid for not going to college (university) (it is an agreement that everyone had to sign who all are applying for thiel fellowship. he/she will not go to college (university) for 2 years. so they don't have to waste time going to college. For the next 2 years they will focus on building their company). It has fascinating questions which no one has asked him before. like what is your contrarian view which everyone feels contrarian but it not so much (yaani ki aap kya aisa sochte hai jo sbko lgta hai ki galat hai aur aapko lgta hai ki shi hai). If you have unlimited money, which problem do you want to solve in this world? anti aging problem, building better roads in the world or what you want to do.questions were incredibly good. He used to get so much happiness in giving the answers to all these questions, then he thought that even if he isn't selected at least he will be happy in giving the answers to all these questions, if anyone reads them. Then he had done something good in life. applying doesn't hurt him.

After applying he got a bunch of interview calls or you can say there were a bunch of interviews that started happening.

There were interviews from senior leaders, product leaders at facebook, twitter and so on.he was getting excited to meet those people.even though in his heart he had no expectation of getting expected.(means usko lg raha tha ki interviews hai kar lete hai jitenge waise bhi nahi).

One day he gets this call saying that you come under top 40 students who are being called to the united state (us) for pitching.

4 days later here is your flight ticket to come to the united state (us).and out of 40 people 20 will get selected to become a thiel fellow he still felt I would not make it or win.

He was very much excited but wait wait buddy he was not excited about becoming a thiel fellow. He was actually excited just because he was going to the United state (us) for free (they had sponsored him) and he felt that he had never got to travel to the united state (us) after that.

He was amazed and thankful to have that opportunity so he applied and of course he went to the US. This was his first international flight he could get on; it was the first time he used his passport. It was the first time he went to San Francisco (San Francisco is the mission district). It was an incredible experience for him because it was also the first time he got exposed to such incredibly smart people across the world.and He was thankful that he was chosen as a fellow among 40 students.

He became the first Asian resident who became a fellow. After that he got 1 lakh dollars. This was his first funding without any stakes.

He was very much grateful to them and more than that he realized that fellowship was a great opportunity. Because you get exposed to some of the sharpest entrepreneurs in the world. And among these He learnt some exciting things or valuable lessons which helped him to build oyo.

Peter thiel and ritesh agarwal

Q- Did he have oyo idea before fellowship, during fellowship or after the fellowship.

- When he came to know about predictability he decided to fix it. And it was the period between Oravel and Oyo. oyo just started and Oravel ins was of course running.

How he came to know about thiel fellowship.

He came to know about Peter Thiel for the 1st time when he was in senior highschool. He was watching this movie called social network and in that he saw this person (peter thiel) writing the first check for facebook (that is $ 500,000 with exchange of 7 % of ownership shares). He thinks to himself about how amazing it would be if I ever get the opportunity to meet him (Peter Thiel). This guy seems to be incredible. So he went to a nearby cyber cafe because he did not have internet access at the place he was living in. At that point of time, he had to go to a nearby store where people could use the internet and so on. And there he started searching about him and then he found the thiel fellowship website. but before him there was no other indian or asian resident who had become a thiel fellow there were of course asians in the united state (u s) who became thiel fellows.

I have added some best scenes from the movie "The social network movie without any spoilers.

social network : I don't want to be a spoiler but I can give you some intro about this movie so that you can understand easily. Basically this movie is based on how Harvard students (mark zuckerberg) create social networking sites (The facebook). which is transformed into facebook. This biggest contribution was given by sean parker.

Sean parker and mark zuckerberg

**Peter thiel investing $ 500,000
(that blue shirt guy)**

Image 1 = here Sean Parker and Mark zuckerberg waiting for their first investment in the company.

Image 2 = here Peter Thiel invests $500,000 with exchange of 7% of ownership shares.

NOTE = These characters are not real, they are playing roles just in this movie (actors).if you want to know then you can search them on google or any searching platform or wait let me attach their picture peter thiel image i have attached already.

MARK ZUKERBERG

SEAN PARKER

How he convinced his parents to go to the United States.

He felt he would not make this fellowship so he told his parents that he is going to the United state (us).there are very nice people who are paying for his trip.

His parents reply that it's fine if you are traveling there just because some person is paying for your trip.

After that soon he became a fellow; they actually put it out in the press so the Indian press started covering it in local languages. So his parents read that and called him at that time he was still in california.

Ritesh parent's - ritesh you won some fellowship this is the matter of prestige and honor.

Ritesh - yes but i will not go to any university after that.

They were very happy and excited about him

But a couple of times later his mother says that ritesh you don't want to do physical university can you do correspondence. (because in India people used to take correspondence degrees).Then Ritesh explains to his mother that he had promised that he would stop out of university for 2 years.

But after some years our honorable prime minister (Mr. Narendra Modi) said,

Mr. Narendra Modi - whenever i listen to ritesh it feels like why did a tea seller not want to be a hotel chain owner this was on live television and his parents were proud of him.

So that day his mother sent a message saying i think it's okay for you not to go to your university.

Comment : parents are the biggest supporter or biggest supporting pillar in our lives. They stood with us no matter what the situation or circumstances were. they will always support us but to gain that support we have to prove ourselves in front of them. For example if you want to start a gym then of course you have to take permission from them. Most of them will not be happy with your decisions but when you go and hit the gym with discipline regularly you and your parents will definitely see the results after which force you to go to the gym. Overall, parents are there to support us but for that support we have to prove ourselves in front of them.

FELLOWSHIP MENTOR

During the thiel fellowship program Ritesh got an amazing opportunity to get mentorship from the foundation's network of tech entrepreneurs,investors and scientists. This includes the likes of facebook founder mark zuckerberg, google founder larry page, tesla founder elon musk, napster founder and serving as the first president of the social networking website Facebook sean parker and and peter thiel himself.

LEARNINGS FROM THIEL FELLOWSHIP

Here are the lessons he had learnt from thiel fellowship.

1) **Being able to do innovative thing**
2) **Thinking extremely big**
3) **Naivety (bholapan) is good**
4) **Value of talent**

Let me explain or elaborate his learnings in an easy way.

1) **Being able to do innovative thing**

   - During thiel fellowship he learnt from other co-entrepreneur that building something new is very important and if you see oyo they are unlike other companies where any one can say that they are an emulation of such a company or copied from any other country. It was purely a new concept and idea that came from India. They are a unique company solving a local problem that was never solved by anyone. This is such a large problem that other companies are copying oyo from outside India. Overall oyo is the original seed or idea that came from India.

2) **Thinking extremely big**

When Ritesh was growing up (solving the issue of predictability) his startup. so He started his first guest house in Gurgaon.

He used to say that he wanted to build the biggest chain of guest houses in the south city area. People used to laugh at him. They used to say that you wanted to open the biggest chain of guest houses in the south city area. Do you know how big the south city is ?

But on the other side when Ritesh was in us (during thiel fellowship).

He met young entrepreneurs who had not yet started their company but their first idea was to build the world's biggest flash storage company.

So thinking big does not come with your background (background like where you came from, are you rich, who are your friends etc)it does not matter.

Overall if you are thinking in any way think extremely big because it does not cost you money,time or effort and of course when you are executing you should look at your resources.

3) Naivety (bholapan) is good

You should be naive to begin with but you should not end up being naive (bholapan).

One of the podcast ritesh had said that

If I knew 20 % of today or if I knew how difficult this business is I would never start this business. I thought that the accommodation industry was very easy. And I have read it on the internet. and it is also a big problem so i thought lets do it.but after starting i came to know how difficult it is to convince hotel owners, opening bank accounts and so on.

ritesh had faced these difficulties one by one when he was building his company but if he knew all about it he would never have tried also.

(km pata hota hai toh acha hai. km se km aisa lagta toh hai ki hum kar lenge) because at that time we don't know how hard it is or how risky it is.

overall naivety is good in the beginning but you should not always be naive.

4) Value of talent.

It is a very important lesson from a business point of view or starting your own company. For 6 months Ritesh ran his startup or his company with 2 guest houses. When he added abhinav sinha who is his coo (chief operating officer) of oyo rooms.after that his company added 20 more assets in a period of 60 days. Which means one good person can change the trajectory of your company completely and it's your job to share the ownership, responsibility, credits everything with them. The value of that is you can be 100x more impactful than what you would have thought.

ABHINAV SINHA

HOW THIEL FELLOWSHIP HAS HELPED HIM

- It helps him from the perspective of exposure.
- It helps him to learn from incredible business people and entrepreneurs in the silicon valley.
- It also helped him to introduce some incredible people in the sector of business.

SOME OF THE BIGGEST LEARNINGS FROM PETER THIEL WERE

- Start small, nail it and then make it big
- Be humble, be focused and have grit
- Focus on your organization's culture, recruit only the best
- Look for details and keep the big picture in sight
- Stay agile, but always remember your mission
- Set processes early on and challenge the status quo
- Work with investors you respect
- Gun for a great product, everything else will follow

RITESH'S EXPERIENCE FROM THE THIEL FELLOWSHIP

The Thiel Fellowship is a school of learning like no other. I was the first resident Asian to be selected and graduated from the Thiel Fellowship, and was mentored by Peter Theil himself along with other visionaries. I learned so much from spending time with a number of U.S.-based startups, famed Silicon Valley entrepreneurs, investors, thinkers, and visionaries. The mentorship I received and the quality of ideas I was exposed to were easily on par with the best business schools. I got to learn everything while actually pursuing my dream.

Learning by doing, that's what Peter Thiel wanted each of us to focus on. Building and scaling a disruptive startup, while simultaneously pursuing the fellowship program, were two intertwined journeys that were also life-defining experiences for me.

"I wanted to fix this problem by using design, technology and talent. That's how OYO was launched in 2013, with the promise of delivering chic well-designed stay experiences"

The most important learning, however, was understanding how to think big and scale a business, and the importance of believing in my ability to create an impact. As entrepreneurs, we are wired to take risks, we are eternal optimists and I learned how to channelize this in the right direction. After returning, I single-mindedly focused on building OYO Hotels & Homes with a mission to upgrade all forms of real estate and deliver quality experiences. I am humbled to see the impact we've made in such a short span of time – OYO Hotels & Homes is today India and South Asia's largest, China's and the world's second-largest, and the fastest-growing chain of leased and franchised hotels, homes and living spaces.

THE REALITY OF BUSINESS

when he came back to India to go to sign a 3rd hotel reality hit him again.Where he realized that the 2nd hotel owner doesn't care whether you are thiel fellow. wheather silicon valley entrepreneur knows you it doesn't matter to them they only care about his profit (mujhe choka munafa kitna hoga) so you can learn from the fellowship but at the end when you when you build your business you have to check the reality that you have start from ground zero (ground level) all over again.

COMMENT: how many books you have read, how knowledgeable you are, maybe you are a college topper or how many prizes you have won. Many times It doesn't matter to people whom you are working with. The thing only matters to people is does it create any values in their life or in the business point of view whether this idea is profitable or not.

WHAT YOU HAVE LEARNT NOW, MAKE SOME NOTES SO THAT YOU CANNOT FORGET

CHAPTER 4
INNOVATION BEGIN'S

"BUSINESS HAS ONLY TWO FUNCTIONS MARKETING AND INNOVATION"

WHY HOSPITALITY ?

As many of us know how the hospitality industry in India works I can not provide you with original data but according to Forbes in 2015 India had about 1 million rooms in its unorganized hotel sector if India had 1 million unbranded rooms in 2015. so this data will be more than 1 million in 2013 when oyo was launched and this entire category is owned by people who have a different full time business and they all had enough cash to build an assets so that they can generate an extra income by giving then to lease, converting them into hotels (dharamshalas) or after 10 years they can sell it also if it is needed.

That's the main reason why Ritesh wanted to start another business in this hospitality sector.

MOTIVATION BEHIND OYO

The motivation behind starting OYO services came when ritesh parents took him to kumbh mela which was held in allahabad (prayagraj) and there he found some chacha ke friend typ like door ke Rishtedar and there he did not have control over the TV remote at his so called relatives home. He wanted to watch cartoon networks while other relatives insisted on watching soap operas. This problem gave him the idea of a separate room with a private TV and full control over things.

APPROACHING AND GETTING REJECTED

The first hotel was the hardest one for him (ritesh) because for someone to trust to say that my whole property is yours I will also improve it and give (handover) it to you. the pricing, content technology, everything is done by you, there is no issue from my side.he also knows that it was quite hard for somebody to believe. He approached many hotel owners with his idea and said I will make it profitable for you but no one believed him.They used to say I was running this business for many years. If I cannot make it profitable then how can you make it ? People didn't believe him at that point of time because he was too small in front of them. As many of you know, a man whose age is 40 or 50 year's how he can believe the guy whose age is just 19.

FIRST PARTNER

He went to the property of rajesh yadav where he had stayed when he was traveling. It is located in south city 1 area of gurgaon in c block so ritesh offer to him was business one on one means munafa hua toh dono ka nuksaan hua toh mera.

Rajesh said to him that it was best deal aap jaise log hamare paas pehle kyun nahi aate the. Because he felt shayad papa ke paise hai 2 ya 4 mahine jalayega aur bhaag jayega he did not believe that this hotel could make any revenue at all because he had less than 20% occupancy and his property was mostly used in weddings.

Rajesh gives his property by saying i don't have faith in you but i will try with you although my occupancy is 10, 20 percent, I don't think it will be a big deal and anyway, I don't see any loss in it. After seeing some growth in his hotel he used to say that ritesh you know that this hotel is empty all the time. Do whatever you need to do but get me some returns because I have a factory to run in Rajasthan. as i have said that 80 % of the unbranded hotel owners backgrounds earned a lot more money by doing something else and hotel us just additional side earning. ritesh replied to him that i will standardize the property and i will make a lot of money for you after listening this he said ritesh you know what you wanna take your brand you wanna do standardization do whatever you want to i will make no money today whatever i make that is an incremental revenue for me in 10 months while operating that hotel he innovated how global hospitality is today being copied by outside the india.

MEETING ANUJ TEJPAL

When oyo started it was not him, anuj and a few interns running it.

Anuj has been a part of oyo since its inception. He was an iit bhu graduate who reached out to ritesh when he had just started oyo. Ritesh knew he could not afford someone from an iit and told anuj so. but anuj had probably seen the potential of the company and agreed to join without salary asking for ESOPs (employee stock ownership plans) instead.

Today anuj is worth a few hundred crore

The risk he took with oyo was big and appreciating.

"There is no art of finding such people. you have to keep meeting new people until you feel that click. Sometimes that takes many months or if you are lucky that might not take even a week''

- **RITESH AGARWAL**

Ritesh also says that you must have a strong sense of gratitude and mutual respect towards each other is crucial for a team to ensure the success of a startup. This positive dynamic ensures that everyone on the team feels valued and appreciated for the unique skill contributions they bring to the table. In addition, having complementary skill sets can help the team work more efficiently and effectively towards their goals.

Q- Who is Anuj Tejpal ?

Anuj is a ceramic engineer from iit bhu. He has more than 8 years of experience in startups across education, hospitality,and consumer internet technology industry.

When oyo was started, Ritesh and Anuj both distributed their work. Anuj's job is to bring property to Ritesh and Ritesh's job is to rent it on the internet.

He is appointed (Anuj Tejpal) as the Global Chief Commercial Officer, OYO effective September 1, 2020. He would be responsible for driving global delivery of revenue for hotels, including overseeing revenue and OTA management, along with direct demand. We've made some significant improvements in our revenue and growth organization in the recent time and with Anuj at the helm, we are positive that these will emerge as our pillars of strength in the future where it would be imperative to preemptively address the needs of our guests and partners.

Anuj is one of the founding members of OYO and was previously the Global Business Development Leader. He is among the core leadership team that built OYO as we know it today. In the last 7 years, Anuj advanced progressively and took on bigger mandates, challenging assignments and has emerged successful each time. In his most recent role, he helped set up the OYO China business from the ground up. He has now passed on the baton to Gautam Swaroop, the recently appointed CEO for the company business in China, while continuing to be the Chairman of OYO China.

Before OYO, Anuj was a Partner at Grassroot, an education company and co-founder of VidyaTimes.com an e-learning portal.

Anuj tejpal (GCCO)
(Global Chief Commercial Officer)

" **A startup is not about money. It's all about value - addition, not valuation. And you should have that passion in you forever** "

- ANUJ TEJPAL

TRANSFORMING HOTEL AND ROOMS

First of all he searched online to see which property was the top most one with budget.

He saw that all of them had good photos and interiors. So he improved the quality of the hotel by adding room services and beautiful photo frames, changing the beds, light bulbs, water jug and whatnot.

The white interior was replaced with warm lights and 2-3 coats of paint were applied in the rooms.

After that He started going to sadar bazaar (like a local market) and bought things which were very very cheap, beg, borrowed, stolen and everything possible in 35000 rupees got the property (hotel) into some basic conditions like deep cleaning, removing bunch of furnitures which was not required (terrible condition) and so on.

STARTING HIS FIRST HOTEL

He puts the oyo in signage on the hotel in huda city center (it used to be called ins earlier) for close to 3.5 months he used to do everything at that hotel from housekeeping staff to sales and ceo.

- He was the guy who was transforming the hotel
- He was the guy who was doing f&b

    Q- what is f&b ?

    F&B stands for **food and beverages** in a hotel the f &b department is responsible for or the members of the f&b services team are required to perform a wide range of tasks which includes :

    - Preparation for services

- Greeting the guests
- Taking their orders
- Maintaining food and service quality
- Food costing
- Managing restaurant and bars
- Setting the bills and performing various other tasks after the guest leave

- He was the guy doing front office work or front office manager (check in check out and cleaning responsibilities was taken by him).
- He was the guy who was spending time with the guests and so on.

" Every time when you are building a company you have to be the first subject matter expert. There is no option other than that "

- RITESH AGARWAL

COMMENT: Maybe you have a question in your mind why Ritesh used to spend time with his guests or why does he perform this type of boring activity ? because the best consumer in the world they know their customer like no one else it is because they are so related to them that's the reason he spend time with his customer that he may know their feedback so that he could improve his mistakes and provide his customers with a great living space on a budget.

STRATEGY TO ATTRACT CUSTOMER

He used mainly two strategies to attract the customers are :

1) **Building strong human values**

2) Introducing technology

According to ritesh businesses in india specially the experienced businesses are not built just on technologies (ritesh has introduced technology in the hotel which i have covered in the next paragraph) they are built on real human values. so they did something very very interesting to attract customers and make their hotel unique.

For every floor in a hotel all the variables like toiletries, linen, notepad, pen, water bottles and wifi etc. It takes 10 minutes to be kept at various places because toiletries need to be kept at the washroom. pen and paper need to be kept at the corner of the other side of the room. They basically did something very unique. They brought small bags and in those bags they kept toiletry items, pens, pads, water bottles etc. They said to their customer that every time when you check in we will give you that bag.There were more than 40 things like this. so that their customers have predictable experiences and hotel owners can generate profits. If both of them earn money (hotel owners) and save money (consumers / customers) then they (Ritesh, Anuj) also end up making money.

They (Ritesh and Anuj) started the hotel with close to 15% to 20% of occupancy and they sold those rooms nights for rupees 999 by using dynamic pricing. Earlier the hotel's Price was flat Rs 2000 for a year.

to kill the competition in the market, Ritesh said the first 3 rooms will be sold at just Rs 999. many of you had heard of the scheme of oyo when he came that is starting at just rupees 999 Because once the volume increases as you see on the internet by popularity or by quality or by price you can sort the hotel.

Ritesh used to sort by price so that he can get 3 bookings first by which the hotel can be in top rank by popularity and Then the price will become higher.

Plus one more benefit it has is if someone stays at Rs 999 and they get the value of 2000 so they will definitely provide good reviews by this his hotel will also be in top in reviews and it was almost like a big thing for him With his dedication and determination the hotels occupancy increased substantially. In a week or before the end of first month the property of rajesh yadav was selling 90% plus in occupancy rate everyone started lining up outside the hotel.

" Always work hard to make sure that your product market fit is well managed "

- **RITESH AGARWAL**

that one property occupancy of 90%. the owner making more money and brand being out there (oyo).Were the 3 things that they felt were the little basics that they had to set before they could go and sign up more properties.

After that they started getting at least 6 to 7 calls a day saying 'hamari property laga doo ji' for them this is the best time ever they were like we are in the right place all the hotel owners love us. We should go and talk to all of them. They started signing properties and started learning stuff.

RELAUNCHING ORAVEL STAYS AS OYO HOTELS AND ROOMS

When they had transitioned from Oravel to Oravel ins customer got confused in between both of them they used to asked them what Oravel do and Oravel ins do so they had decided to keep a separate name oyo stays (on your own) Oyo started running a lot then they shut down Oravel. so Oravel was transformed into oyo rooms in May 2013.

The logo for oyo was inspired by lord puri jagannath the two " O " s in the logo resemble the eyes of the lord and the " Y " is the nose the image will make it more clear.

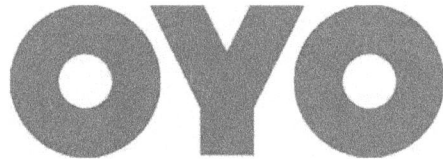

INTRODUCING TECHNOLOGIES

They launch tablet at their hotels where every check in 100% oyo check in happen by the tablet and i will come advantages of that it is very similar to how the ola drivers side app works every time when you get into the car it say pick me now by means of which you know which location, what time, which k,m.

from where the customer boarded and what time he checked out. They also audit their hotel every 3 days by a Geolocation app which gives them real time pictures of a room so they literally merge the feedback of guests.

One stayed in room number - 103 who checked in by the tablet along with the feedback of their audit manager who had gone to room number - 103 along with the audit request that he came up with and many other things on the technology side they had done.

PROBLEMS AND SCALING UP

He had faced problems while signing the 3rd hotel or you can say the big roadblock happened in the 3rd property very early.

When they realized that alright now we know how these 3 properties / hotels work but how do we take it to the 4th property because everything was being practically managed by them (Ritesh and Anuj) there was absolutely no scalable proposition they had in a business they were almost like any other guest house chain operator.

So how do they changed that to a large scale business

They (Ritesh and Anuj) were having a great life from these 3 properties they used to make 1 lakh rupees each as net revenue.They used to earn 3 lakh and out of that they used to spend Rs 2 lakh and from leftover Rs 1 lakh they Used to bring new property/hotel. According to them it was a great life with no problems. And they were thinking, " What more needs to be done now? Will keep buying one property every 3 months. Life is good.

It was the same time when Ritesh became a fellow and he got the opportunity to go to the US (United states) and there he learned 2 major things.

1) **Thinking really really big**
2) **Ensuring that you build innovative products**

After that he came back to India and spent a lot of time ensuring that they built processes and systems. but in all of this before the processes and systems. what they had gotten right, how do they make sure an entire life cycle of a property / hotel would operate.

- Sign up property / hotel
- Standardize it
- Sell it
- Ensure that you deliver a great experience every time

Those were the 4 basics that they had learnt and that is what got them ready for the next generation of growth for their business.

" whenever you are starting your business get your shit in order make sure that you know what are the 3 or 4 magic things that you have and focus on doing just those 4 things and not many other items "

- RITESH AGARWAL

FIRST FUNDING ROUND

First time Ritesh tried to reach out to so many people and almost everyone said that it gonna not happen. Basically, he felt that probably it may be his background. He doesn't come from any universities and he was too young. Also at that time, this can be the reason why he was unable to raise capital (money).

he felt he will build a business which makes money at the end of every month and he would take those earnings and reinvest them in the business and probably he went to banks, vccs, angel and so on in the early days he was not the guy to fundraise he had 2 rounds in both he had very unique experiences

1) Angel round
2) Institutional round

The angel round was very special. He was running 2 hotels. Both hotels are making at 35% margin at the end of every month. they are making decent money which would afford their living and then whatever money they would save for 2 to 3 months they would invest in the 3rd property that was their mission but then they were Parallely reaching out most of the Vccs and they are all mostly pass saying that you know not a very exciting situation but one point of time suddenly on angel list which is angel.code where you can apply for funding from a lot of angels.

He got the opportunity to speak to light speed. Light Speed was the first institutional investor. They do a lot of diligence before they invest so they come into hotels (saw the hotel), they meet the hotel owners, they met some of their customers.

Ritesh feels all these things are good because he was getting to learn a lot from these questions that they were asking from them because all of these ventures folks have a lot of experience.

One day they get a call saying that you know we want to really be partners with you guys and you want to be partners for the very long term here is a financing opportunity.

here is discussion with ventures and ritesh

Ventures asked : what is the amount you wanna raise

Ritesh : Ritesh and Anuj did a lot of math. Their math says 50 lakhs.but they were scared saying 50 lakhs because its a huge amount. so they asked for 50 lakhs with a lot of fumbling.

Ventures : 50 lakhs is too small a check size for our size of funds here's our offer and we would like to offer you and it was a few crore in capital (money) is it okay for you ?.

The first question comes to Ritesh mind was will be able to, initially, Ritesh was afraid he felt if he raise this capital how will he return it back because a bank gives you 10% of return in a the year this is high risk capital this expectation of return from them would be much higher as well. but he guessed they had a lot of conviction in themselves, they had great belief in their partners and they had belief in them at light speed and they have been together since then.

Ritesh is very happy to share that they have given very remarkable returns at least on paper.

BUILDING OYO - PRENUERS

The first year they grew from close to 3 properties in the early January 2014 towards the end of the year when they grew too close to 40 properties in gurgaon alone.

" choose your beloved ones very well "

- RITESH AGRWAL

From January to March was a tough time for them. They were all struggling to grow and they were adding hotels too. people were starting to know them. These properties are filling up left, right, and center. Venture capitalists had started calling to them (phone call) they never thought that venture capitalists would ever come to them.

So the first 3 months were very tough. but they are still struggling because they have a lot of hunger and passion to grow. Everything was there in their business/startup but they could not grow it because there were some fights like every day when they tried to sell their rooms to a customer There was a call coming back. Sir, the housekeeping valve ran away, the staff is not cooperating with us, and so on.

" When you start your startups/companies you will go through a lot of these big challenges where you have this reality check

Remember you should be very excited when these things happen. you should feel like you are going through the best period in your life because a lot of people run away from these problems. You should be very excited about these problems "

- RITESH AGARWAL

There was demand from customers and hotel owners were ready to hand over their hotels but they didn't have the staff to manage so many properties. He discussed this problem with many people and asked them how we should solve it. Everyone said build a good team. He approached Bejul Somaia

(Bejul Somaia, Managing Director, Lightspeed Venture Partners) for the same. Bejul told him that:

" Bringing one right person could change the fortune of a company. He told Ritesh that the best CEOs spend 40 % of their time meeting great people and bringing them on board and then letting them do what they want to do"

- Bejul Somaia

Ritesh Agarwal and Bejul Somaia

And then Ritesh thought about how to get more people so he started using and writing on linkedin. A few people come forward to met him and most of them looked at him and they would be like where is Ritesh? He says I am Ritesh. At that point in time, he was too young with no beard (soft face) at all so no one joined them. It was a bad phase for them and almost all of them felt that they would take advantage of him in some way or the other because they felt he was a young boy and might not be very smart.

Initially everyone thought that Oyo is a real estate business. which made it difficult for the company to get engineers.Or you can say that no engineer was ready to join them. so he flew to Bangalore and tried to make them understand that Oyo is a technology - driven company. However, he managed to convince them and flew back with 3 or 4 engineers. Because what he was trying to do was very difficult to understand, people were saying this guy is very young so he might not be very smart.

MEETING ABHINAV SINHA

During the thiel fellowship ritesh was told not to trust 2 kinds of people

1) Consultants
2) People who are mostly like those who have emigrated to the US and are staying there.

Interestingly in his tough time, there was one guy called Abhinav Sinha who was recommended to Ritesh by his close friend whom he trusts a lot.

Abhinav went to Harvard Business School (for MBA) but right after that joined BCG and worked for 5 years. so he was qualified for both of the parameters consultant and was in the US.

Ritesh said : it makes no sense to meet him yaar I was told not to trust these kinds of people.

Ritesh's friend : you have to meet him. He is really really a good guy.

Ritesh : OK fine

There was a property that they had signed but was not transformed (meaning oyo's job is to transform the property into oyo standards) and in a terrible shape. So Ritesh sent him the same property to check. what he will do now Ritesh feels that american hai (he is from America) he will realize how tough this business is.

Abhinav called Ritesh 2 hours after check-in to the property/hotel saying aloo ke parathe yaha bahut ache hai ritesh.

It was the first time when Ritesh started feeling good about this guy because he was not complaining at least.

Abhinav said : Ritesh, let's break things between both of us.

you will own

- Supply
- Brand
- Sales

And I will (abhinav will) ensure that these properties are well operated and well standardized and we will have good questions between each other. There will be accountability but it is our responsibility, and we will fight for it. When we leave the room we will trust each other on these decisions.

Ritesh said: great sounds good

Anuj said : I will own the supply

So 3 of them as a team when they had started and that one year was absolutely amazing since then Ritesh can credit these 2 people and of course, the great team they have brought together across the company.

LITTLE INTRO ABOUT ABHINAV

Abhinav Sinha is the Global COO & Chief Product Officer at OYO. Abhinav was previously a Principal at The Boston Consulting Group from October 2009 to June 2014. Prior to that, they were an Associate, Clinical Affairs and Business Development at OmniGuide from January 2008 to December

2008. Abhinav started their career as an Assistant Manager at ITC Limited from June 2003 to May 2007.

Abhinav Sinha has an MBA from Harvard Business School and a Bachelor of Engineering in Chemical Engineering from the Indian Institute of Technology, Kharagpur. Abhinav also attended DAV and St.Thomas schools.

Abhinav sinha (coo)

STRATEGY TO GROW

They were the largest player by the end of 2014 in Gurgaon. So Ritesh had said everything is going well in one city.

- Let's make it big
- Let's take it across the country

Which was the time to grow and this they have started discussing in mid of 2014 and the question comes.

Q - what do we need to be ready for the next expansion?

Q - why do we expand?

Q - what is the strategic value of expanding?

If you get the first 1 lakh rooms you get it without any cost because there were no cappics or you get it faster because there were no cappics and whoever gets this first 1 lakh room most customers will come to them Because in the budget segment there is no other good supply that is available.

Once customers are there with you, the rest of the lakhs of room owners (let's take a random number of 44 lakh) will invest in the properties for which brand the brand brings customers to them.

So they decided that they want to get 1 lakh rooms in the next year. Do what makes it.

By the end of the year they felt the next 6 months 2014 mid when they said.

This is the strategic reason why we will scale next year, they said.

Q - what do we need to be ready for it ?

"Bring people who are ready to stick their neck out for the mission of the company "

- RITESH AGARWAL

For hiring there was a very simple ask: anyone who comes and joins them he / she should be able to do anything for the mission that they are all aligned for.

So they had decided in the 6 months they would do 2 things.

1) They will build a very strong hiring roadmap (so that when they want to grow they need better people).

2) They will innovate a bunch of technologies (to make sure that next time when we are doing things. things are idiot proof)

HIRING STRATEGY

A lot of people in a first team when they hear them ask them. How did you build this team ?

Their way of doing it was : The first 60 people were hired by the leaders who were hired by the Ritesh.

First leaders hired by Oyo or cxo's (chief experience officers) of oyo.

Ayush Mathur : chief supply officer (global)

Ayush joined Oyo in 2014, and since then has reimagined how OYO grows and operates. Under his leadership, OYO catapulted the pace of onboarding properties while driving a cultural change on the supply side. He enabled the business model shift to full-stack franchise business (SMART), which has contributed to the organization's success since 2016. Many key OYO platforms and capabilities that exist today are thanks to Ayush and his team. These include ORBIS, remote account management, remote BD set up, CO-OYO app, SAM teams, and several franchise contracting fundamentals for asset partners.

Ayush has also continuously recruited, mentored, and supported global teams and talent (like Manu Midha, Shirish Damani, Abhishek Bansal, and others). He also helped Abhinav and Ritesh in building a grounds-up local team that launched their Indonesian market in just 2 days.

Ankit Mathuria : chief technology officer

Ankit Mathuria is an OYO's new Chief Technology Officer and a key member of the OYO CXO group. Ankit comes with 15+ years of in-depth technical knowledge in consumer-facing industries. Ankit joined oyo from Amazon where he has spent the last 7+ years in multiple businesses with his most recent stint as CTO for Souq (now, Amazon. ae, an Amazon subsidiary). He is credited with launching and growing Amazon in the UAE and KSA, and scaling Souq Egypt. Ankit has helped grow the technology organization across 4 countries with the right organization structure, engineering, and operational excellence. Throughout his tenure, Ankit built multiple core platforms to solve critical business problems. He built an export and compliance platform to launch and expand the Amazon Export business; built a solution to make Arabic bi-directional compliant and launched the Arabic experience. Prior to Amazon, he had successful stints with the Royal Bank of Scotland as Vice President of Market Data and Algorithmic Trading with IBM India Software Lab as a Hardware Virtualization Engineer. He brings in global working experience, having spent time in the US, India, Singapore, London, and the Middle East.

Even before Ankit started with Oyo, he began to interact with OYO hotel partners. His biggest focus is to provide better technology experiences for Oyo hotel/home partners and his mission is to make OYO a leading technology company of choice by building products from India for the world.

Abhinav Sinha: global coo (chief operating officer) & chief product officer

About abhinav sinha i have covered in the last paragraph you can read.

Kavikrut: Chief Growth Officer

The company's vision is to continue to grow OYO into a global direct-to-consumer brand with communication

narratives that their guests, partners, and public at large can relate with and be further inspired by. This goal demands a strategic focus with well-planned execution across several key functions. And to enable this, they are bringing their global communications team and brand team together under one of their CXO members, Kavikrut. In addition to his current role, Kavi will also directly work with Global Brand and Global PR/Communications who will both report to him going forward. Given the significance of India and South Asia in OYO's overall story, Rohit and Kavi will closely partner together to make both the Brand and PR teams successful.

Kavi most recently has been involved on key initiatives with the Product team and was leading their OYO LIFE business in Japan. He has been at OYO now for 6+ years and as the Chief Growth Officer, has in the past launched the OYO Home and OYO Life businesses. Back in 2016, he built their early teams in the revenue, and marketing, brand, and PR functions while in his first year at OYO, he led OYO's expansion to 100+ cities in India.

Gautam Swaroop: Ceo, Oyo International

Ritesh is thankful to Gautam for his exceptional leadership in China, which is recovering strongly from the pandemic. In China, their RevPar is back to 74% of Jan 20 (pre-COVID) levels at 20% higher ARRs and significantly increased gross margins. Today, Oyo has 2000+ hotels in China and consistently adds thousands of rooms per month. More importantly, Gautam and his team have consistently delivered on their biggest priority of ensuring high partner and customer satisfaction.

Abhishek gupta : CFO (chief financial officer)

Abhishek Gupta is the Group Chief Financial Officer at OYO. He is responsible for driving the financial strategy and provides guidance for long-term strategic planning and execution. Prior to OYO, he spent over two years at Philips India as CFO for Home Lighting business division. He has also worked with General Electric in various senior finance roles in different business verticals like Energy, Capital, and Healthcare in India and abroad. A Chartered Accountant and a MBA from Indian School of Business (Class of 2010), Abhishek was also a part of the Executive Management Program at Harvard University.

Maninder Gulati : CSO (chief strategy officer)

Gulati, a chemical engineer by training, might have gone all melodramatic but his passion for Oyo was real. One of the earliest board members of Oyo, Gulati joined the Gurugram-headquartered company as its chief strategy officer in October 2015.

But for Oyo founder Ritesh Agarwal, Gulati was a guardian and a mentor to a 19-year-old who had famously become Masayoshi Son's chosen one overnight, with his Softbank Group leading a $100-million round in the company the same year.

Over the next six years, Gulati would be the moving force behind several decisions taken by Agarwal, with Oyo expanding to more than 43,000 hotels with over 1 million rooms in around 800 cities in 80 countries at its peak.

Dinesh Ramamurthi : CHS (chief human resources)

He is the Global CHRO at OYO Hotels & Homes. At OYO Hotels and Homes, Dinesh is responsible for hiring leaders across the world, setting up the right culture, creating a meritocratic and performance-driven organization and making OYO the most aspirational workplace across the world.

He (ritesh) sat together with them and asked for the list of 20 smartest people they have ever met in their life, worked with, and so on

And recommend it to me.

Then first 60 people from their network with valuable experiences from across some of the biggest manufacturing and retail companies in India and abroad were hired by those recommendations.

After that oyo hired numerous leaders and executives who are best in their fields and different regions. Interestingly, the team of leaders from IIMs, IITs, Harvards, and Ivy leagues colleges with rich industry experience led by the young college dropout.

How to find the smartest people ?

This question was asked to Ritesh; he replied (Ritesh replied) back by saying that there is no science to find good people; it is a brick by brick process. you have to keep fighting hard long enough and there will be the light at the end of the tunnel.

CREATING WORKING - CULTURE

At oyo ritesh called himself as CCO (chief clarity officer) which means his job is to make decisions on what to do and advise what not to do by setting out these principles which enables everybody to decide how they can do their job.

" Team that share a strong camaraderie and are bound together by the same vision will enable a startup to grow and become sustainable "

- RITESH AGRWAL

He focused on building a strong workplace culture from the beginning. where he created a listening culture that encourages everyone to share their opinions.

As Bejul Somaia advised him to bring smartest people on board and let them do what they want to do and taking inspiration from other successful companies Ritesh has deployed a distributed leadership model at oyo which makes the organization democratic in its functioning. distributed leadership is about delegating decision-making to a broader group letting employees own the problem you want them to solve empowering leaders to own and drive parts of the organization while retaining a strong management core.

While building the team Ritesh noticed and learnt about the young generation that they (young generation) want to work for a vision which is more than just two meals a day. They look for ownership to make decisions, be accountable and create an impact.

Inder ritesh leadership, oyo has established a team of thousands of employees and partners who are dubbed as ' Oyo - prenuers ' and are encouraged to take ownership of their own projects.

The Company regularly highlights the stories of oyo-preneurs who are driving the company's success.

SUPPLY PLAYBOOK

Most companies in India are built out of jugaad rights. jugaad in the sense jugaad on both forms they build their company they had a very clear view of saying that they will do jugaad to innovate but after that, they will build a strong process.

Playbookisation means taking small innovations and building them fully idiot proof so they build a very strong play book. The supply book was as under.

- They knew which location they should go to because there was a lot of demand.
- They knew what price to sign the hotel at because you know the room would sell at that price.
- They knew what kind of owners to partner with.

So they used to in early days by city decide which city they will partner with own property

Owners and which city they will partner with the rented property owners.

The reason is owned property owners are willing to take a price hit but will spend time to analyze and operate the property.

Rented property owners will not take a revenue hit but will spend time to operate the property so cities where they were stronger as the customer experience brand they said only owned property.

In cities where they felt they needed an even stronger partner, they said only rented property. A lot of these things are codified which means tomorrow when the supply guy went on the ground to sign hotels he just had to take a play book. This entire process ensures that they are ready for scaling up. ritesh had also done a bunch of other things but of course, this is a big difference between growth hacks vs product market fit that is making sure.

Initial days do the jugaad but great companies take that jugaad and build it into a process that operates like a machine that just keeps churning stuff out.

WHAT YOU HAVE LEARNT NOW, MAKE SOME NOTES SO THAT YOU CANNOT FORGET

CHAPTER 5
OYO THE UNICORN

"WHEN YOU REALLY WANT SOMETHING, THE WHOLE UNIVERSE CONSPIRES IN HELPING YOU TO ACHIEVE IT "

TIME FOR EXECUTION

They built what they called internally a cannon to go out and take any Freakin country and win that country as a part of product and experience. somebody came and told them about zo rooms (Zostel's zo rooms). Zo Rooms (Zostel's Zo Rooms) was the competitor of Oyo Rooms. They effectively did exactly everything they were doing in the initial days.

So one saturday afternoon when this news came about they saw them getting all their property live ritesh called his entire leadership and everyone was angry.

Never use that cannon to take a bird out, use that cannon to take a large animal out they had built this massive capability.

- They had a playbooks of recruiting
- They had a playbook of signing
- They had a people across the country

All they needed to do was use their capability really really well.

Next Sunday morning at 10 AM the entire office was called and they were closed to 100 people there.

Ritesh asked randomly to the people how many properties can we sign in the next 1 month. Give a random number some said 35 that was the maximum, somebody said 26, somebody said 31 and so on. Ritesh said we are gonna add 100 properties next month which is a 5 times jump. people were there. They were like this guy has gone mad, another young entrepreneur losing his mind but then came the most interesting part.

Ritesh shared the team's full plan of how they were going to add 100 properties and the plan was as under. They're gonna add 100 properties in Delhi alone and this is a way we're gonna do it.

Basically, he created a 7 cluster. In each cluster, they are gonna have mini trucks with these 12 items each hotel needs for standardization. signing will be done in one morning next morning audits will be done 3rd morning mini trucks will come to put stuff up and 4th morning they gonna stuff life.

There was ownership decided by cluster in each of these areas. That's when people started feeling ok. He has not lost his mind, he knows what he is doing makes sense. What came after that was one of the most amazing things their company has done.

They launched this plan which they called MI-100 and they have funny names for these projects in the company. It was the mission impossible 100 they signed 130 properties that month MI was done across the country they did it in every dam city in this country. signed 4.5 thousand hotels and there is particularly no number 2 in our business as of date.

LAUNCHING APP

They started working on their mobile app in March and shipped the first version of it on 22nd April, 2015 on the Android Play Store. The iOS version went live on 1st May 2015 on the App Store. For the last few years, they have refined, added more features and when they launched the app it grew to over 2 million downloads in less than 7 months of its launch and a significant share of their business now comes through it.

INTENTION BEHIND THE APP

OYO Rooms came into existence to solve the problem of predictable and affordable stays. They knew that it took a lot of effort to find a good hotel at pocket friendly prices and they wanted to make it easier for consumers to do so. They did it with their offline product – they partner with selected hotels, standardize them, and make them available at great prices – and they wanted to take it further with their mobile app product. They wanted to build an app that could get the hotel booked in (almost) no time and make it feel effortless.

HOW THE APP WAS DESIGNED

I will share some of the choices they made with the hope that it can benefit some more people in the product and technology ecosystem. They would love to hear feedback from us so that they can improve it and work on their flaws.

1) Shorten the booking funnel – Our app allows you to make a booking in just 3 taps (if you want to book a hotel near you) including the tap to open the app and cuts down on the booking steps and time over other hotel booking apps. We laid down an interesting internal target of 50% of the new users to cancel the booking immediately after making one – the booking flow had to be this seamless that people didn't realize they just made a hotel reservation. When we released this to the customers, we got some customers who were pleasantly surprised by it and some who got shocked by it and panicked when they saw they had made a booking while just playing around with the app. We took this feedback and added a little delay in the booking creation process and prepared the customer for what was to happen next through some subtle animation and provided a way to cancel the next step if they chose to.

2) Mandatory Sign-up/Sign-in – This one was the most controversial choice. Conventional wisdom told us to remove any steps that came in letting a customer explore the app and browse the hotels. However, we wanted to separate the sign-up, data entry, and user authentication steps from the booking flow to retain the seamlessness of the booking experience, even for the first time booker. To mitigate the impact, we tried to make the sign-up process simpler by eliminating the need of a password and using One Time Password (OTP) as the authentication mechanism. We ran some exciting offers for our first-time users of the app and made sure that we didn't lose many customers from the top of the funnel. It is important to look at this approach with respect to the context of your business. Ours is a transactional heavy business where most customers download our app when they have a need to book a hotel. If you are building a game or a utility app, the same approach may not work as well there.

3) Payment is to be done post booking – This was a deviation from the norm again. Most sites/apps (including our web app) for the payment step into two and ask for a choice between paying now and paying at the hotel. The drop-offs at the payment step on the mobile form factor are quite high in India (given our internet speeds and the second-factor authentication for payments). We decided to make this into a linear flow by first creating a confirmed booking for the customer and then providing an optional step to make a payment.

4) Dynamic Home Page – Our home screen is not a booking widget and we don't presume every time you open the app, you are there to make a booking with us, especially when you already have a booking with us. We believe it is our karma to help our customers get a better stay experience and we want to support them at all steps – booking a cab, finding nearby restaurants, ordering room service, etc. Our app's home page is a card-based layout where you can see your bookings and get some quick action buttons (relevant to your booking state) along with options to search and the nearest OYOs shown upfront without the need to search.

message from ritesh about their app

We have tried to innovate with some purpose and made some choices that may not please everyone, but at the same time get a lot of customers to love us and differentiate ourselves from others. We believe in continuous experimentation and improvement and we know there's a lot more to do. I am proud of the young team that has worked on our app and gotten it to here and am equally excited about the work that does underway to make the booking and stay experience of our customers even more seamless.

GROWING UP RAPIDLY AND ENSURING THE SYSTEM IS RIGHT

Early part of year 2016 they saw their customer experience and happy percentage were starting to drop they knew for a fact that they were never going to let it reach a place of no return because there was a percentage they always had in their mind so early part of the year 2016 when they were the largest hotel brand had large revenue they said they will continue growing but big focus area for the next 6 month (in 2016) is to get their house in order.

They were going to ensure great guest experience across the country in that 6 months (of 2016).

I will tell the matrics they were tracking

1) Unhappy percentage
2) Trip advisor scores

So the trip scores in 2014 when they were in gurgaon alone was 4.1 when they grew nationally it started dropping from 4.1 by the end of 2016 it was 3.7 which is not bad but also not great so the early part of 2017 they said now it breezed their target unit and for this year (in 2017) first 6 months they will just build their company to ensure each of their guests has a great experience and I will tell you what the flip is. they were seeing this number they knew they had to get right but they needed a push. There was a facebook post a customer had put up which went viral and it talked about a few hundred shares which was a bad experience for oyo.

they did 3 basic things

1) Get your promises right

Which are AC, WIFI networks, hygienic lenin etc. A lot of these things they generally said to their customers.

2) Ensure that the technology is adopted end to end of the hotel so check in happens very easily.
3) Delight guest

Interesting update in the last 7 months of 2017 customers who are top customers who stayed more than 20 nights a year with them have increased by close to 40 % their trip advisor scores at an average of 4.4.

Trip advisor just go to noida and searched search guest house in speciality login they were the number 1 in both bread & breakfast and specialty login and not just that of these categories of the top 10 ranks 8 are dominated by Oyo and these unhappy percentage have decreased by more than 50% in that 6 months.

The reason behind saying this is to always maintain a healthy balance between consultation and non-consultation you will always have this period you will run really really fast anyone of you who is a marathon runner who knows this you sprint but then you are at a place where you say that okay let me get some juice let just jog for a while. Let me make sure that I'm gonna survive until I enter the race and once you are alright then you Freakin sprint like there was no tomorrow.

ADVERTISING, PROMOTING AND MARKETING

In the starting phase of building the oyo the marketing was done by word of mouth. after that when oyo became popular. Ritesh started to follow new strategies because he was facing some challenges.

" Marketing is a contest for people's attention "

- Seth Godin

The biggest challenge was to direct traffic to the associate hotels, because if they did not get traffic, they would have pulled out and the entire model would have flopped. OYO is a mass brand but a large part of its audience is not tech-savvy.

Yet, at the same time, the brand has to register in the minds of all age groups.

To start with youngsters and then society as a whole, the team made OYO's presence felt across a lot of college campuses and partnered with wedding planners, event managers, convention centers, and banquet halls. To engage millennials, OYO capitalized on digital marketing and built a vast and loyal following on various social media platforms. To connect with its audience at a deeper level, the team created multiple short videos and films. One of the videos, Independence Day, which featured Bollywood actors Manoj Bajpai and Raveena Tandon, fetched over a million views for the brand. Furthermore, OYO launched multiple short films that depicted travelers expressing themselves freely in the comfort of a hotel room. The brand also launched a high-impact online campaign #oneforeveryone, encouraging consumers to share their quirky hotel moments.

To bring traffic to the OYO app and create viewer engagement, OYO partnered with the reality show MTV Roadies, which is extremely popular among the youth. While the contestants of the show enjoyed the best hospitality experience at OYO, the brand ran an OYO Roadies contest on its app. Five lucky winners got the opportunity to meet the show's famous host-Bollywood actor and celebrity Rannvijay Singha-and win many exciting prizes. The campaign involved a 360-degree marketing approach where the contest was promoted via paid media (TV and Voot), owned media (CRM, banners on the OYO app) and social media platforms, and earned media (PR). The campaign led to a significant increase in performance metrics, like contest participation, a high click-through rate of

push notifications, and social media engagement. To target user bases in different parts of the country that are not exposed to the MTV Roadies kind of content, the company runs many localized marketing activities. As an example, the team created bright red paper cups that would resonate with OYO's logo. Every custom paper cup distributed ran with the slogan 'Book an OYO in 3 Sips', and urged the beverage drinker to download the mobile app. These were branded paper cups were distributed in shopping malls, corporate offices, colleges, railways, and bus stands. Also, the company runs the OYO Brand Ambassador program, in which selected college students to create awareness within their circles, run campaigns in the college, manage hospitality for their college events, and bring in bookings for OYO. In the process, they gain essential skills in marketing, communication and leadership.

To increase its brand visibility and transaction, OYO has created exciting partnerships with over 2,500 brands, which are mission-oriented like OYO and have high user traffic. For example, OYO has partnered with SARVA, one of the most promising yoga and wellness startups. It is funded by an illustrious list of global investors, which include names like global pop icon Jennifer Lopez, Bollywood diva

Malaika Arora, and American baseball legend Alex Rodriguez. SARVA has set up wellness studios at select OYO Townhouses to enrich the wellness experiences of every customer. OYO has also partnered with ZEE5, India's fastest-growing OTT platform. Through this partnership, OYO offers its customers fantastic discounts on a ZEE5 subscription, and ZEE5 subscribers enjoy discounts when booking rooms via OYO.

Similarly, OYO has partnered with Airtel and Amazon Pay to launch OYO Stores on the Airtel Thanks app and Amazon Pay that enable customers to book quality and affordable accommodations. Along similar lines, OYO is creating some great campaigns with its partners and offering integrated services to travelers. OYO has also extended its offerings through its partners like MakeMyTrip in India and Ctrip in China.

OYO has multiple brands. To offer the right brand to the right customer segment, the team relies on a data science system for proper segmentation and targeting. This process helps reach the right set of customers with targeted messages. Every campaign is customized based on audience needs, preferences, platforms, and business goals. The team continually keeps experimenting with different segments and takes customers' feedback on whether they like the brand's communication and product offering. This feedback eventually feeds the company's marketing, product, and customer experience strategy.

Ritesh says, 'Every overnight success is a five- to ten-year-old journey. Over the years, OYO has invested in building relationships with its stakeholders, like customers, asset owners, partners, influencers (including YouTubers and bloggers), and journalists by following three core principles-transparency, mutual respect and, above all, reminding each other that they are in this ecosystem for the long run. The stakeholders have not only appreciated the great product and services OYO is offering, but have also shared constructive feedback when required. Starting from Ritesh, OYO's global team is always on top of things. It owns relationships and nurtures them. Today, the word of mouth of customers, influencers, partners and earned media contributes a lot to OYO's growth. By September 2019, OYO had hosted over 11 million guests with a 90 percent repeat rate.

TIME FOR EXPANSION

After a successful expansion in India Ritesh thought to expand it to other countries also. Ritesh's point of view on expansion is that he believes that fundamentally other countries are also facing the same problems as India, a large scale of unbranded units (hotels) where the quality of experience is fundamentally missing and because there is no single large brand that ensures this the demand side is also missing so by keeping in his this huge problem of unbranded hotels he thought to expand in other countries.

EXPANSION IN MALAYSIA

In 2016 they started their first expansion with Malaysia and from there they got great feedback and their business has been growing consistently there.They had learnt some valuable things from their first expansion and they took those learnings for their next expansions.

EXPANSION IN NEPAL

At time ritesh saw nepal was having a huge amount of travel from India as well as southeast Asian countries.

In May 2017 Ritesh launched Oyo operations in Nepal Kathmandu because he has always been a fan of Nepal as a country which has a combination of religious tourism.

Nepal is the country which is present in the bucket list of so many people and he felt it's one of their Neighboring countries so they thought of expanding in Nepal.

Soon after launching oyo in nepal their occupancy is running from 85 % to 90 % occupancy rate since then they got lots of love from that country.

EXPANSION IN OTHER COUNTRIES

After launching successful expansion in Malaysia and Nepal. Ritesh had enough data and learnings to manage international markets.

After a lot of research and analysis, oyo established operations in the international market. (like the US, UAE, INDONESIA, CHINA VIETNAM, SAUDI ARABIA, PHILIP,PINES, JAPAN and so on).

Now Oyo is operated in more than 80 countries with 1 million rooms across 800 cities.

LAUNCHING OYO TOWNHOUSE

OYO Townhouse is based on the needs of the millennial traveler. Every single element of the hotel – from the breakfast menu to the booking process has been re-engineered for comfort, efficiency, convenience and affordability. Each Townhouse is designed to complement its neighborhood.

WHAT IS OYO TOWNHOUSE ?

A whole Flat/building is converted into OYO which gives a homely atmosphere and a comfort of a hotel at the same time. The staff is friendly and there are vibrant colors and theme based rooms.

A light green painted room will have light green colored curtains and a same colored bean bag - overall cute, decent and comfortable rooms at best prices. (Free OYO KIT with biotique products is cherry on the cake)

The Kitchen can be in house or they have got tie ups with the city's best restaurants and food is delivered quickly.

Oyo townhouse offers complimentary facilities such as :

- Breakfast
- Water bottle
- Free wifi
- Laundry service and facilities
- Disabled access
- Air conditioning
- Television
- Fitness center
- Drawing Room café
- Conference room
- Whiteboards
- Free printer, business services, and magazines
- Tour/ticket assistance

- Dry cleaning/laundry services
- Free newspapers in lobby
- Luggage storage
- Wedding services

Oyo townhouse also offers complimentary insurance which include :

- Accidental death coverage up to INR 10,00,000
- Baggage loss coverage up to INR 10,000
- Accidental medical expenses coverage up to INR 25,000
- OPD treatment

How to claim insurance

Steps on how to claim Insurance

On OYO App/Website:

- Open your OYO App and go to 'My Bookings'
- Select the particular stay that you want to claim for from the list of stays
- Click on the 'Insurance' option from your stay details page
- Select the type of claim, follow the next few steps, and your claim will be registered with ACKO

On ACKO.com

- Go to www.acko.com & login with your mobile number registered on OYO
- Under the 'Claims' section, select OYO Claims which opens your 'My Account' page

- Select the 'Stay' filter which opens all your stays
- Select the particular trip, click on the 'Initiate Claim' button below the Policy details section
- Select the type of claim, follow the next few steps, and your claim will be registered with ACKO

This unique offering is aimed to benefit their customers as well as their asset owners. Insurance cover will help improve customer experience and satisfaction and thereby lead to higher repeat rates and increased yield for the asset owner.

LAUNCHING OYO OS

In 2017, OYO launched OYO Townhouse, a mid-market brand at selected locations for premium customers. In 2018, the company saw significant expansions to China, UK, and Indonesia. The same year, OYO established OYO OS to incorporate technology to simplify operations for property managers.

They launched their Hotel Management System for the web called OYO OS. It is now used in over 25 countries around the world. OYO OS facilitates an OYO Hotel Manager (HM) to manage today's check-in, checkout, room prices, and property performance. He can also check his total earned incentive in real-time.

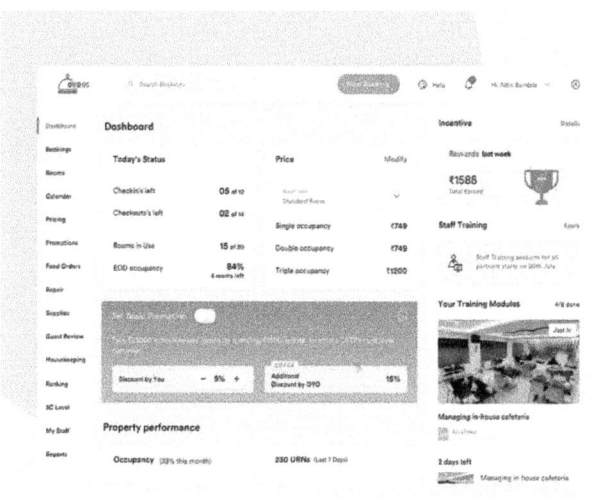

OYO OS is a free hotel management solution (HMS) designed for Android devices by OYO. This software is a unique and innovative platform that offers a wide range of features that can significantly reduce costs, increase profitability, and prevent fraud. It also ensures efficient operations and delivers an impeccable guest experience. OYO OS, hotel managers can easily manage their hotel operations from anywhere, at any time.

The software provides a user-friendly interface that is easy to navigate. The platform is designed to help hotel managers manage their inventory, track bookings, and manage housekeeping, and oversee financial transactions. Additionally, OYO OS offers a range of features that can help hotel managers improve their guest's experience, including guest check-in and check-out, room service, and in-room dining.

Overall, OYO OS is an efficient and innovative hotel management solution that can help hotel managers streamline their operations and provide an exceptional guest experience. The software is free to use and is available for download on Android devices.

OLD BUSINESS MODEL

Oyo started as a hotel aggregator and used to lease some rooms and sell them under its brand name. Ritesh used to acquire some rooms from hotels Because these were mostly properties that had low occupancy rates. Due to this, the company was able to get these rooms at a very low price. After that, Ritesh used to invest some money in these rooms to standardize and use technology to manage the rooms and optimize their utilization to make them better than before. After transforming the rooms Ritesh used to co-brand them with the name of Oyo and rent it out in the market (through his website before the app was launched and when the app was launched these properties were listed in the app) to generate earnings from them and Apart from this, all the services that had to be provided to the customers from check-in to check-out were handled by OYO staff only.

But when Oyo's operations were limited to limited places and the size of the company was limited, it was easy to give the same experience to the customers. However, as the company was expanding, the company was facing the problem of finding its own team. Basically, it was the same team that managed the customers from check-in to check-out. At some places, this service was quite good and at some places, this service was quite bad. And this was the differentiator of the quality of service, which was gradually increasing as the size of the company was increasing.

Let make it clear with an example :

When a food chain company tries to expand on its own, its service quality changes a lot, that is why most of the companies try to operate on the franchise model so that the quality does not change much during expansion.

The same had happened with Oyo also, at the time of expansion there was a lot of difference in the service quality of the company. And Oyo's business advantage depends on 2 things.

1) Low price

2) Good Customer service

so it becomes very important for them to perform their business on both these parameters.

The biggest problem was that they used to take 10, 15 rooms under themselves and then they used to give the full price for the whole month to the hotel owners and when they used to sell these through their website or app they used to give discounts on some rooms.

Due to which some hotel owners used to do fake booking because of this oyo was facing loss.

Flaws on old business model

1) Service quality issue

2) Asset light model but not so light

3) Fluctuation in property prices

NEW BUSINESS MODEL

By facing all these kinds of problems. In 2018 Ritesh decided to change his business model from hotel aggregator business to the full stack asset leasing and franchise model. It is the Same model in which McDonald's, Pizza Hut, Domino's Pizza, and other food tech startups used to work. At the same time, Ritesh brought the same business model to the hotel industry, which he used to bring the entire hotel under his control.

He and his team used to control everything by themselves like.

- Kitchen
- Hotel cleaning and transformation
- Staff training
- Rooms

And so on

By applying this franchise model Everything was under their control so that they could set up the entire customer experience as per their convenience and keep the customers happy. i know i know now the question that will arise in your mind is that :

Q- why ritesh had not applied this business model before?

Applying this model is not easy because It costs a lot of money operationally, it is a very capital intensive process because everything has to be managed by Ritesh and his team. Hence the cost increases a lot.

WHY THIS BUSINESS MODEL IS BETTER THAN OLD BUSINESS MODEL

As we all know that before launching his new business model Ritesh had created a solid brand value of this company. although this business model it has merits and demerits

By the way, this business model is better than the old business model because it is :

- Asset light
- Less employee expense
- Less dependency on property price fluctuation

By this model oyo used to provide and take:

- Its brand with hotel partners
- Oyo used to take 15 % to 20 % commission on sales. In some hotels, the commission is 15%, in some, it is 20% and in some cases, the commission is even more than 20%. It depends on different factors.
- Asset light

Problems they are facing in this model

- Lack of control
- Dynamic pricing

Just like the prices are changing in airlines, Oyo will also change its prices according to the demand, but due to this dynamic pricing, the hotel owners of Oyo are not very happy. And this communication gap has also been created between the company and its partner.

How companies deal with these problems it's upon them but By the way, this new business model is much better than the old one.

HOW THEY TRACK CUSTOMER BEHAVIOR

They do this by leveraging technology to drive efficiency, reduce friction, and even predict customer behavior. This is where data science plays a critical role. Their data science team constantly gathers insights and feedback to make the OYO.

At OYO, every decision they take is to drive a stellar end-to-end customer experience. They do this by leveraging technology to drive efficiency, reduce friction, and even predict customer behavior. This is where data science plays a critical role.

Their data science team constantly gathers insights and feedback to make the OYO experience more personalized and consumer-centric. The idea is to understand what exactly the customer wants and how they can best deliver it to them.

While analyzing data, the common questions they ask are –

Q- Who is our customer?

Q- What do they want?

Q- How can we help customers find their stay better ?

Q- Where and why will we open the next OYO?

The answers to these and a number of other questions help them understand their customers better so they can provide their customer with a more personalized, near-customized experience.

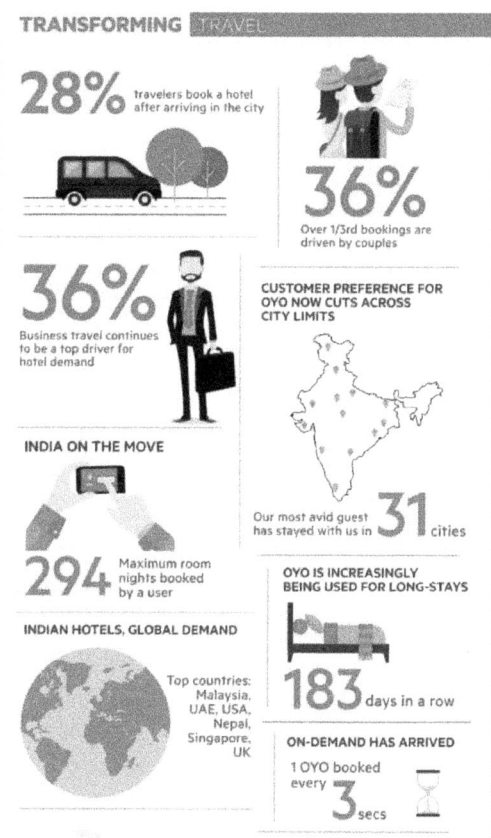

INFOGRAPHIC

LAUNCHING OYO WIZARD

They at OYO Hotels & Homes have a firm belief and passion to deliver real moments of magic to their customers. They launched the OYO Wizard, one of the largest paid hospitality loyalty programs in the year of 2018 and since then through their multi-brand approach have offered curated offerings for the changing needs of the travelers. they are pleased to announce that in a span of two years OYO Wizard has reached the 7.5 million + member mark as of May 2020.

This indicates a 50% growth in subscribers in the year 2020 over the base last year. The program has been designed to recognize and reward frequent customers by offering them a unique host of benefits, including guaranteed discounts, cashback, discount coupons, and upgrades.

In view of the current scenario owing to Covid-19 and reduced travel, they have extended all Wizard memberships by 4 months at no additional cost and have contributed all proceeds from the Wizard membership purchases for April 2020 to the OYO Welfare Fund. The OYO Welfare Fund was set up for the benefit and welfare of the employees & asset partners and their staff members impacted by the pandemic or the consequent restrictions all over the world.

As India returns to normalcy OYO Wizard's growing subscriber base serves as an important indicator of the growing need for affordable and flexible choices with end-to-end customer experience management. Keeping in mind the changing needs of customers in the post-pandemic world, they also recently launched a customer-centric initiative, OYO Wowcher that offers customers double its value with the flexibility on the duration of redemption.

Commenting on this milestone from Abhishek Bansal (Vice President – Revenue Management – OYO Hotels & Homes)

"We are proud to announce that our loyalty program OYO Wizard has crossed the 7.5 mn + mark. Even during tough times like these, this milestone serves as a testament that our offerings are in line with our customer's requirements which have a new benchmark post COVID with flexibility & affordability being at the core. As we shift gears with Unlock 1.0 and hotels re-open in a phased manner, we strive to offer our loyal customers exclusive curated deals for hygienic sanitized stays with convenient, seamless booking options at industry-best prices."

It is interesting to note that over 60% of our hotels on the OYO platform are a part of the Wizard network and 60% of all transactions made by premium Wizard members done on Wizard member hotels, resulting in higher revenue for Wizard partner hotels as compared to non-Wizard hotels. On the OYO platform, every second room booked is by a Wizard member with a 2x+ lifetime spend as compared to non-wizard members.

At present, OYO Wizard is available across 4 tiers – Wizard Blue (INR 99 for 6 months membership), Wizard Silver (INR 199 for 1-year membership), Wizard Gold (INR 399 for 2 years membership) and OYO Wizard Lite.

Core benefits of premium tiers include –

- An additional 5% discount on all Wizard member hotels (over and above existing discounts)
- An additional 10% on Wizard Base hotel selected by the user
- Instant OYO Money rewards worth INR 500, INR 1200 and INR 3000 for Blue, Silver and Gold respectively

There are benefits provided to members in the higher tiers, including 40% discount vouchers (1 for Silver and 2 for

Gold) and OYO Money cashback on every stay (INR 75 for Silver, INR 200 for Gold).

MAKING IT TO UNICORN

In September 2018 OYO got itself listed in the list of unicorn companies after it raised $800 million from SoftBank.

Ritesh Agarwal has praised the development of 100 Unicorns in India, but warned that valuations are only temporary.

Ritesh posted a video message on Startup India's Twitter page, Ritesh says,

"We are sprinting towards glory to make India the largest entrepreneurial ecosystem in the world."

- Ritesh Agarwal

He continues to say that he believes that this is just the start, and as the startup ecosystem matures further, Indian entrepreneurs and startups are going to take the world by storm.

In a standalone tweet responding to the video message, Ritesh said,

"I am bullish on Indian entrepreneurs taking the world by storm. Founders should remember that valuations are temporary, values are forever."

- Ritesh Agarwal

RITESH AGARWAL TWEET

Ritesh Agarwal
@riteshagar

Not just a milestone but a stepping stone that lays the path for the next 1000 unicorns. I am bullish on Indian entrepreneurs taking the world by storm. Founders should remember that valuations are temporary, values are forever. Focus on doing good & stay grounded.

> **Startup India** @startupindia · 09 May 22
> "We've crossed the milestone of 100 unicorns from India, I want to congratulate the teams & entrepreneurs behind this success... We are sprinting towards glory to make India the largest entrepreneurial ecosystem in the world"

Ritesh is one of India's earliest and most-well known unicorn founders, having started his hotel aggregator business in 2012. This was rebranded to OYO Rooms in 2013 before Agarwal had even turned 20, and OYO became a unicorn in September 2018, when it raised $1 billion at a valuation of $5 billion.

ADITYA GHOSH

Aditya had a very successful stint with Indigo Airlines, which became the largest and most profitable airline in India under his leadership. Aditya is a strong advocate for diverse and inclusive workplaces and was the driving force behind Indigo having the maximum number of women pilots and a workforce comprising 43% women. He has also been a part of several CSR programmes focusing on women empowerment, children and education, and the environment. He sits on the Board of Directors of the Nani Palkhivala Arbitration Centre and is a Senior Advisor to the Tata Trusts and helps lead the Cancer Care Initiative of the Trusts.

Aditya studied Law & history from Delhi University and practiced law before joining the InterGlobe Enterprises as the General Counsel. Aditya is a fitness enthusiast and is considered to be one of the fittest business leaders in India. His other interests are arts, sports, traveling, hiking and camping on the hilltops, and he is always keen to explore and try out new things.

On 20th November 2018, he was appointed as the CEO of OYO hotels in India and South Asia. In 2020, he joined Fabindia as a member of its board of directors.

WHEN GHOSH WAS APPOINTED HE MAKE THE STATEMENTS

"I'm thrilled to join OYO's mission of creating quality living spaces, and partner with Ritesh in shaping the company's future in South Asia – a critical growth market for the company. "OYO Hotels is one of the most exciting, innovative, and mission-driven companies, run by an exceptional group of people."

"I am thankful to the board for inviting me into the august group to further build OYO as a global brand to reckon with, by not just growing fast, but growing right."

ADITYA GHOSH (E-x CEO OF OYO ROOMS AND HOTELS)

" If some things are not done or a lot of things are not done, can it get worse ? Yes, it can absolutely get rapidly worse so it is important that everybody gets with it "

- ADITYA GHOSH

RITESH THOUGHTS ON THE ADITYA GHOSH

His business acumen, his problem-solving capabilities, and his customer-centric approach to innovation helped him build an influential brand that is loved by all makes him an excellent choice for OYO Hotels. Above all, his ability to deliver growth with large-scale impact, whether to develop an inclusive culture or give back to society, makes him a great addition to the leadership team.

STEPPING DOWN AS CEO AND BECOMING BOARD MEMBER

Aditya Ghosh was the CEO of OYO Hotels & Homes for India and South Asia from December 2018 to 2019.

Aditya Ghosh was appointed to the board of directors at OYO Hotels and Homes on December 2, 2019.

After a 15-month stint as the CEO of OYO's India & South Asia hotels and homes business, Aditya Ghosh has been elevated to the company's board of directors. He will join existing directors Ritesh Agarwal, Betsy Atkins, Munish Varma, Bejul Somaia, and Mohit Bhatnagar on the company's board.

Hospitality firm OYO has said it has elevated Aditya Ghosh, currently chief executive officer (India & South Asia) for the hotels and homes business, as a member of its board of directors.

In his role on the board, Ghosh will focus on five key areas namely.

- safety and security
- customer experience
- corporate governance
- revenue management
- stakeholder communications

WHAT YOU HAVE LEARNT NOW, MAKE SOME NOTES SO THAT YOU CANNOT FORGET

CHAPTER 6
LOCKDOWN, DOWNFALL AND BOUNCE BACK

"SUCCESS IS HOW HIGH YOU BOUNCE WHEN YOU HIT BOTTOM"

LAUNCHED OYO OPTIMUS APP

A dedicated transformation app enables their on-ground teams to understand the transformation requirements of a building while giving cost estimates and budgets in addition to assigning tasks and tracking the pace at which the process takes place. Insights from Optimus enable a strong on-ground team comprising civil engineers, architects, and designers to transform an asset within 3-14 days and on-board them at an even quicker pace, which is in stark comparison to the industry.

The app supports:

- Collecting room and property level information
- Uploading images
- Getting audit summary and detailed audit report
- Submit the audit for approval
- Updating the status of Transformation tasks
- Tracking the progress of Transformation

Screenshots of app

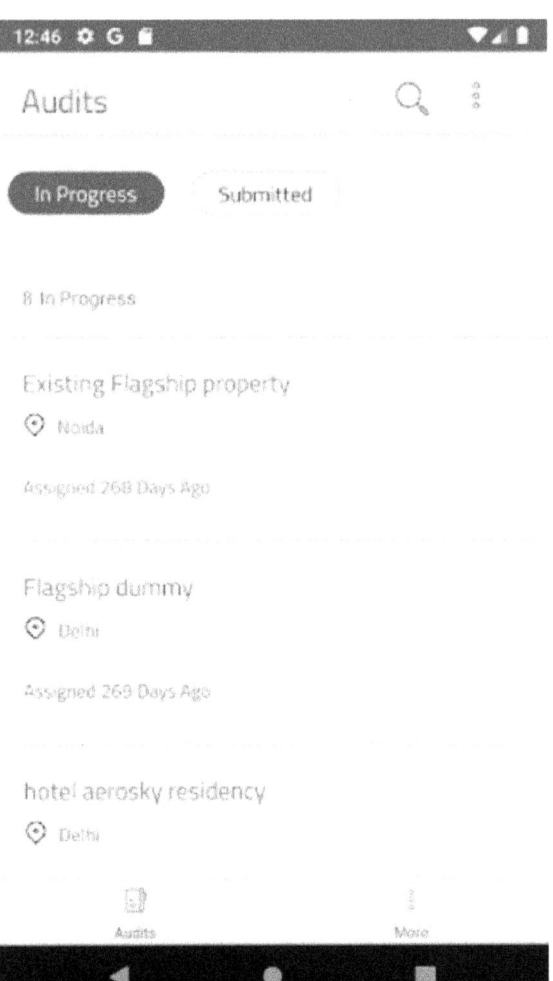

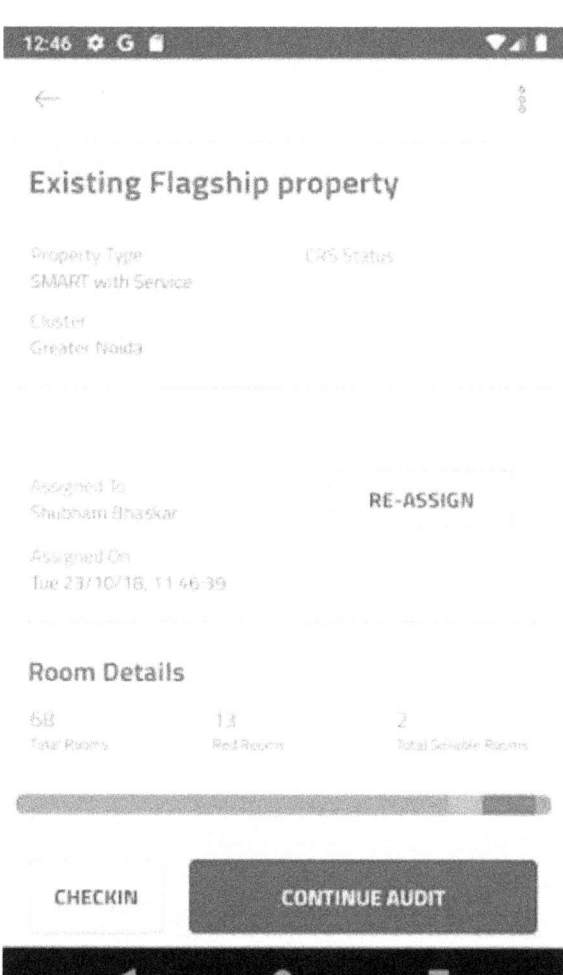

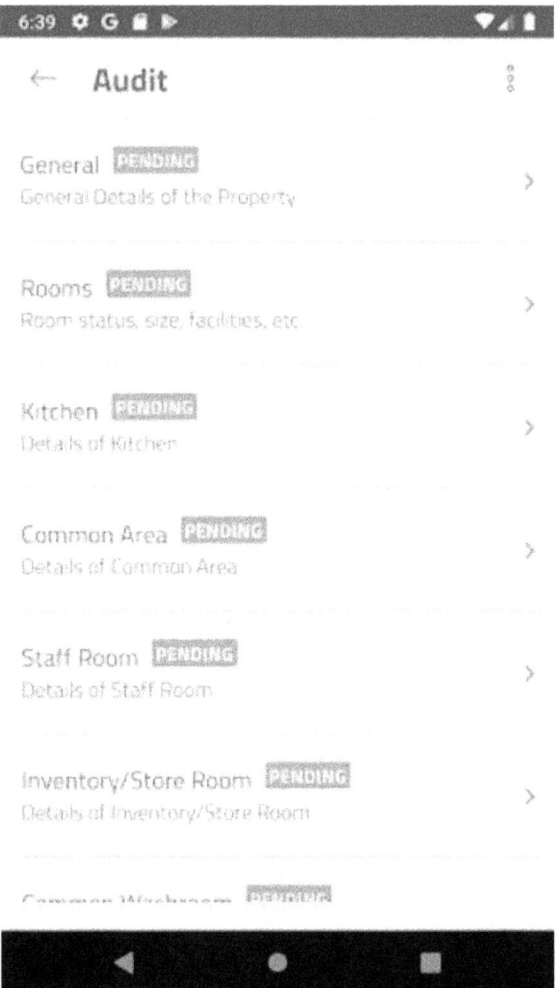

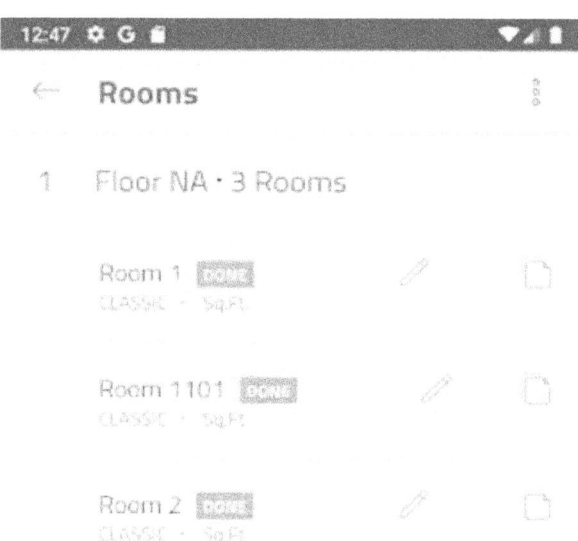

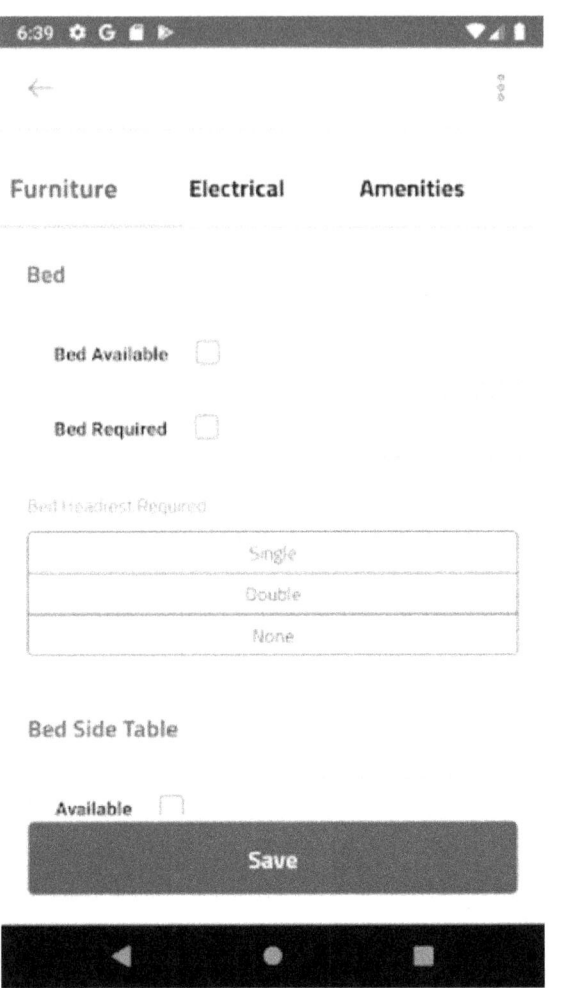

OYO'S Expansion

OYO commenced business operations to address the needs of budget travelers. Thereafter, it expanded its portfolio to target different customer segments. The mid-market boutique hotels branded as OYO TownHouse (OTH), corporate apartments branded as Capital O, Edition O, and

Silverkey, millennial housing branded as OYO Life, upmarket resorts branded as Pallette and vacation rentals branded as OYO Homes (Kavirkut, 2017) became part of OYO's comprehensive market offering. OYO diversified beyond organized living into OYO Workspaces (PR Speak, 2019a) and WeddingZ (Kashyap, 2018).

OYO Hotels and Homes

OYO's flagship venture was OYO Hotels and Homes. By September 2019, OYO had opened its doors in more than 500 cities in 28 states and 9 Union Territories in India. OYO continued to strengthen its presence in smaller cities.

The speed at which OYO expanded rendered the growth of competitors such as Treebo, Fab Hotels Zenrooms, Vista Rooms, and RedDoorz appear miniscule.

OYO Life

OYO ventured into the co-living marketplace in October 2018 with OYO Life. It aimed to provide hassle-free accommodation to millennials (JLL & FICCI, 2019), young professionals, and students. The millennial workforce was a major driver of demand for co-living spaces. In 2018, people aged between 18 and 35 years constituted 42% of the workforce in the top 7 cities of India. In total, 2.6 million of the 4.1 million working millennials who stayed in rented accommodations opted for shared living spaces. The co-living market in India was expected to grow at a compounded annual growth rate (CAGR) of 17% and become a one trillion market by 2023. Although OYO Life was a late entrant in the segment, the market potential was huge. Zolo Stays and Nestaway were other major players in the co-living segment.

OYO Workspaces

Co-working businesses in India witnessed a massive spurt between 2017 and 2019. Gross working revenues doubled to `34 billion during this period (Money Control, 2020). Demand for co-working spaces was concentrated in big cities with Bengaluru and the National Capital Region at the forefront. The price per seat ranged from `6,999 to `8,000 (PR Speak, 2019).

Weddingz.in

OYO acquired Weddingz. in in August 2018 (Kashyap, 2018). The entity provided hassle-free wedding-related services for clients. Weddingz. in's revenue spiked by 480% while the number of bookings rose by an astounding 636% in the first year of joint operations with OYO (Hashmi, 2019).

Table 3. Estimated Demand for Organized Co-Living (Million).[a]

Year[b]	Demand	Realized Demand	% Realized
2018	3.64	0.094	2.59
2019	4.03	0.176	4.37
2020	4.44	0.242	5.46
2021	4.79	0.317	6.62
2022	5.21	0.392	7.53
2023	5.7	0.47	8.25

CO-OYO app

In April 2019, the company announced the launch of the OPEN programme, an initiative for its partner hotels to help them reach their business goals. It further Introduced an upgraded Co-OYO app for hotel partners to provide complete visibility on all business.

The in-built CO-OYO app helps asset owners monitor progress and access payment-related information in one place. Through the Co-OYO app, asset owners can have complete visibility on cash flows, business performance, pricing, customer reviews, and recommendations. The app includes advanced analytics, which enables a deep dive into asset performance over time, an intuitive interface that is easy to navigate and make decisions regarding value-added services, boosting performance by providing insights and easy-to-understand metrics and graphs that allow daily monitoring of performance.

LAUNCHING OYO SKILL INSTITUTE

When Ritesh started his expansion and new ventures he needed well-trained staff. And he was not able to find the quality of staff in the market So for this he set up OYO Skill Institute India.

OYO to set up 26 training institutes for hospitality enthusiasts across India in 2019.

HOW OYO PLANS TO PROVIDE SKILL TRAINING TO LAKHS OF WORKERS

Vikas is a young boy who hails from a small village on the outskirts of Patna. With a dream of providing a happy future for his family, he drops out of school and starts working as a help in a hotel in Kolkata with his uncle.

Similar to Vikas are 3.8 million individuals who are the sole bread-winners for their families. They offer services ranging from room service, and housekeeping to front desk manning in hotels and restaurants. They are the torch bearers of the tourism fraternity and represent the Indian core value of 'Atithi Devo Bhava' for millions of guests.

According to the World Economic Forum's Travel and Tourism Competitiveness Report 2013, India ranks 11th in the Asia Pacific region and 65th globally out of 140 economies ranked as favorite tourism destination. India has been witnessing steady growth in its travel and tourism sector over the past few years. Total tourist visits have increased at a rate of 16.3% per annum from 577 million tourists in 2008 to 1057 million tourists in 2012.

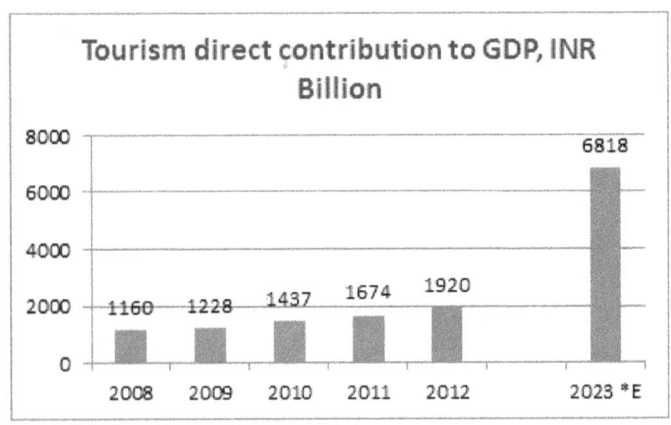

Tourism in India has significant potential considering the rich cultural heritage, variety in ecology, and places of natural beauty spread across the country and thereby it is a potentially large employment generator.

In terms of employment, the travel and tourism sector supported 25 million jobs in 2012, constituting 4.9% of the total employment in the country in 2012. It is expected to amount to 31 million jobs by 2023 indicating huge scope of direct employment.

There exists a forecasted requirement of around 2.8 million employees for restaurants, 4.1 million employees for hotels, and 0.3 million employees for the travel trade segment by 2022 resulting in an incremental requirement of a total of 2.7 million employees for the tourism sector as compared to 2012 employment.

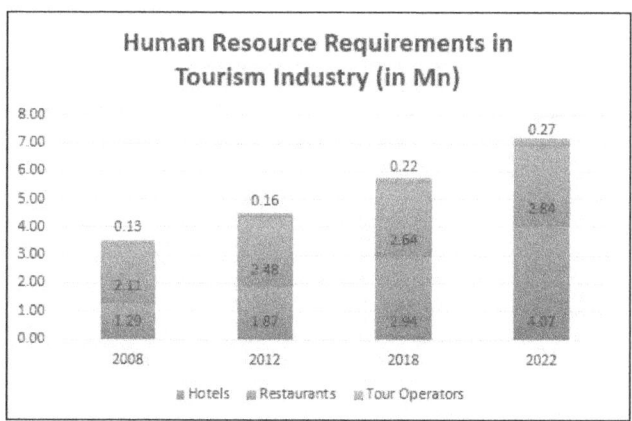

While the tourism sector in India is targeted to grow at an annual rate of 12 percent during 2011-2016, adequate training and skill development infrastructure and hence availability of trained manpower has not kept pace with growth.

The hospitality sector alone witnessed a shortfall of 0.5 million employees during 2011-2012 which is expected to rise to 0.8 million by 2017 and 1.1 million by 2022 as per the target growth levels.

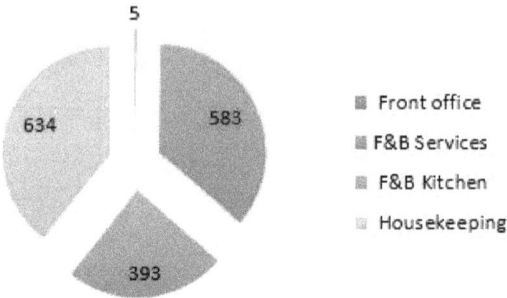

Human Resource Requirements in Tourism Industry (in Mn)

As per a study by the Ministry of Tourism, formally trained managerial staff accounts for only 16% of the total hospitality sector and 21% of the total travel and trade sector workforce. Efforts are thus required to enhance the skill sets of non-managerial staff in the sector.

With 20% of the travel and trade sector employees being casual workers, the development of the basic skill set is important. These include health and personal hygiene, cleanliness, basic service techniques, cooking techniques, garbage disposal, etiquette and manners, basic nutrition values, basic tourism awareness, first aid, client handling and behavioral skills, etc.

OYO Rooms decided to capitalize on this underlying opportunity. With a vision to build a pool of skilled workforce, they intend to up-skill the present staff available in 4,500+ partner properties across India and also provide newly trained staff to the industry.

• An MoU between OYO Rooms and the Tourism and Hospitality Skill Council (THSC), Government of India, was signed to train three lakhs workers across 150+ cities in the next three years at the 4th National Conference on Skill Development 2015 on 27th November 2015.
• OYO Rooms have also been associated with 7 state governments under various initiatives to strengthen our objective to ensure that people employed in unorganized segments can access growth opportunities through up-skilling/reskilling and recognition of prior learning.

OYO Rooms has been accredited by THSC under the aegis of the National Skill and Development Council, Govt. of India, as an official training partner in hospitality.

#OYOforSkillIndia, an initiative from OYO Rooms, is a small contribution to transforming India through innovation. The training and certification will help these individuals regain their identity and open the doors to a plethora of hidden opportunities.

A long-term vision is also to build a professional network of hospitality staff. This will be a significant career move for the workers who meticulously perform on-ground operations and leave no stone unturned in continuously raising the bar for service standards.

MAKING HISTORY

Five years after its inception, Indian hospitality chain OYO joined the unicorn club in 2018. Merely 1 year after that, OYO founder Ritesh Agarwal joined the billionaire club of the country.

According to Hurun Global Rich List 2020, OYO founder Agarwal is the world's second-youngest billionaire. At the age of 24, his wealth was estimated at $1.1 Bn (INR 7,800 Cr) in the Hurun Global Rich List 2020.

Ritesh Agarwal is the second youngest billionaire after model and entrepreneur Kylie Jenner, who amassed $1.1 Bn at the age of 22.

MEETING WITH DONALD TRUMP

During US President Donald Trump's visit to India, he was among the select India Inc businessmen to meet the President.

Agarwal had tweeted earlier in the day about meeting Prime Minister Narendra Modi and during his interaction with Trump, Agarwal introduced OYO as a young startup and said that the company has around 313 hotels in the US. In response, Trump said that he already knew about OYO. Praising Ritesh Agarwal's work, he said, "Not such a small company, by the way. Good job."

COVID-19 PANDEMIC IMPACT

OYO has faced several challenges. But The most challenging period was the covid - 19 due to which Oyo had faced many problems like running out of rooms , hotel owners started boycotting oyo rooms.

In a video message to Oyo employees, the company's 26-year-old founder (at that time his age was 26) (**Note:** this voice message was created by Ritesh during the covid - 19 pandemic) Ritesh Agarwal admitted that its revenues had plunged by "over 50-60%" in recent weeks and that its cash "runway has come under severe stress." In response to this crisis brought about by the COVID-19 outbreak, he said Oyo will reduce "every controllable cost," cut capital expenditure, and abandon its pursuit of acquisitions But Oravel Stays Pvt. Ltd, or Oyo, which had already cut more than 5,000 jobs in recent months, does not "intend" to fire more people, Agarwal reassured the company's 25,000-strong workforce. "Oyo will emerge stronger and more resilient after this crisis," Agarwal said.

In the circumstances, Agarwal's words were defiant—and highly optimistic. After pursuing its ambition of becoming a global hotel superpower for three years, Oyo was facing an unprecedented crisis that threatened to wipe out a large part of its business for the foreseeable future and dent its $10-billion valuation.

OYO had faced several challenges that led to its decline in 2020 and 2021. Some of these are like:

- Covid - 19 pandemic
- Allegations of fraud
- Legal battles
- Competition from other players
- internal turmoil and layoffs

As a result of these challenges, OYO's valuation dropped from $10 billion in 2019 to $3 billion in 2020. It also reported a net loss of $510 million in 2021. It struggled to raise new funds from its existing or new investors amid the pandemic-induced crisis.

Q&A WITH DR MANDAR VAIDYA, CEO JAPAN, SOUTH EAST ASIA & MIDDLE EAST, OYO

Q- What strategies have OYO deployed in Asian countries to weather the COVID-19 storm?

Dr Mandar Vaidya (MV): In this industry, maintaining the trust and confidence of guests is key, and this is reflected in the guest-first approach OYO is taking through our new protocols, in order to provide reassurance and peace of mind to guests.

All aspects of the customer journey especially hygiene and cleanliness are being relooked at going forward. Contactless experiences will be important. We also believe that travelers will demonstrate preferences for hotels, restaurants, and lodging facilities that communicate enhanced sanitation and hygiene protocols. The focus is on being clinically clean.

Technology would also be a factor. As a hospitality company that has invested significantly in technology, OYO is well positioned to leverage this for our partners.

In what ways has OYO been helping key workers and local communities?

MV: OYO is deeply concerned with the spread of COVID-19 and the impact it has on people and businesses around the world. The hospitality industry has been impacted and we are also concerned with the impact COVID-19 has on our partners. Our responsibility as #TeamOYO compels us to come out in full support of everyone connected to OYO as we navigate through this difficult phase.

OYO has identified a large number of our hotels to partner with hospitals for setting up safe, pay-per-use quarantine facilities. Others are focused on providing safe shelter to tourists and travelers who are stranded in certain areas owing to the lockdown for the greater public good.

We have started a fund internally and are also contributing to other external funds to support the fight against coronavirus across different parts of the world.

OYO in South East Asia has set up a dedicated Fund of $200,000 to support our partners whose lives, families, and businesses are infected and impacted by this pandemic. I will also contribute a portion of my salary to this fund.

To support medical and health COVID-19 frontliners in Mindanao, OYO is offering discounts to practitioners from hospitals within a five-kilometer radius of its partner properties. The company is also closely coordinating with BPOs and other businesses for accommodation for their employees and with stranded foreign tourists affected by the lockdown.

In the Philippines, we are offering accommodation at discounted prices to practitioners from hospitals within a five-kilometer radius of our hotels in Mindanao. In response to the need for more accommodations raised on social media and by local government units and NGOs, 24 OYO properties in Mindanao were reopened. We have also worked with the office of the Vice President, Leni Robredo to open dorms for frontliners in Quezon City.

In Malaysia, we are offering complimentary rooms to medical practitioners at three of the busiest public hospitals treating COVID-19 cases in the country. For government employees and those working in essential services, we are offering relaxation of up to 50 percent across OYO hotels. Additionally, we have reached out to embassies and consulates to offer discounted tariffs for tourists and guests who need a place to stay.

In Indonesia, we have opened doors to healthcare front liners from RSPAD Gatot Soebroto, one of the nine hospitals in Jakarta designated as COVID-19 handling facilities. We are also exploring the possibility to extend the free rooms to other designated hospitals in Jakarta. We are also reaching out to embassies and consulates to offer discounted tariffs for tourists/guests who need a place to stay.

We have taken a series of measures to accommodate foreign nationals stranded in the country as well as provide support to frontline medical staff, aircrew, corporates, tourists, PGs, etc. who need accommodation. We reached out to more than 15 embassies in order to support the Ministry of Tourism in efforts to secure shelter for all travelers in need across the country.

OYO stands in solidarity with all OYOprenuers and our partners around the world. Our effort reflects the organization's culture and values, which we hope, would spur others to do their part during this challenging and uncertain time.

Q- Can you speak a little more about the OYO Welfare Fund, and what it has been used for?

MV: Proceeds will be used for the benefit and welfare of the employees at our properties, asset partners and their staff members impacted by the pandemic. In the long run, it will also be used for the welfare of the community at large when faced with such situations.

Through this welfare fund, OYO employees have the opportunity to contribute voluntarily to help those in need. The OYO leadership team and company are further contributing INR 2.5 crore (INR 25 million) to the Indian PM CARES fund to support millions of people with healthcare, infrastructure, and other facilities. The company has made global investments worth approximately $3.5 million or INR 25 crore in the fight against COVID-19 and pledges to continue doing all it can to support those in need.

OYO in South East Asia also announced a dedicated fund to support its partners and their families in the region who have been afflicted by COVID-19. The setting up of the fund for SEA follows a dedicated fund of more than a million RMB in China to support infected employees and their family members.

The fund, set up with a dedicated commitment of $200,000 by OYO in South East Asia, will cover partners and their family members impacted by COVID-19.

Q- In what ways has the coronavirus caused OYO to adapt its plans and strategies for growth and development in the near future?

MV: Our business is constantly evolving and innovating. The pandemic has forced us to rethink and review every aspect of our business and make the right decisions required for its success. We have put together an improved model that promises to deliver better value and greater efficiency to the business. The decision is in the best interest of all stakeholders to maintain business continuity amid the economic pressures.

In preparation to face the protocols of the new norm, we have rethought every aspect of our business and will continue to consider all options that enable us to succeed and contribute towards the success of our partners and the communities we serve. Our goal is to get back to our core purpose – providing clean living spaces at affordable prices – and we will continue to move towards that goal.

Preparing early is key to weathering the storm and I am confident we will emerge in a position that sets us on a path towards long-term success.

Q- Pre-coronavirus, OYO was one of Asia's fastest hotel chains. What do you think explains its success?

MV: SEA is a strategic growth market for OYO globally. We are constantly looking at being a long term wide-scale impactful and sustainable company for our customers, our asset owner partners, our stakeholders and our OYOpreneurs.

Like in India, there was a massive dearth of affordable and good-quality hotels in the unbranded budget hotel category in the region. OYO's success is down to fulfilling the need for affordable, clean living spaces outside of the main cities. Guests trust our brand and we are already known for pioneering effective solutions tailored to their needs.

We are also present in towns and cities where the bigger chains are not. We look forward to strengthening our footprint across the country with a diverse portfolio and relentless commitment towards delivering more choice and delighting our guests with exceptional customer experiences.

We are focused on bringing OYO's successful model of combining design, hospitality, and technological expertise, financial acumen and operational capabilities to real estate owners in more cities and towns in Malaysia, giving them the ability to get a higher return on investments, access easy financing opportunities, transform their hotels, and offer good quality customer service, thereby significantly increasing occupancy and profitability – in every OYO building, with the OYO promise of AC, free Wi-Fi, TV and clean linen for all travelers.

For our customers, we're committed to deliver beautifully designed, chic and comfortable living spaces at hard-to-ignore prices. We are committed to build on the success of our business model and work with small and independent asset owners to upgrade unbranded hotels into quality living spaces and offer them at affordable prices in the best locations across the region.

Q- Do you feel optimistic about recovery over the next 12 months?

MV: The entire global economy is hurting, and OYO is not immune to the effects of this global pandemic. We exist in an ecosystem of partnerships and interconnected businesses, many of whom are feeling significant pain.

it's too early to tell what the impact on occupancy rates will be, but we have studied trends and data In countries who have lifted isolation protocols and we see as many as 90 percent of those ready to travel want to start domestically, as experts point to safety fears and the desire to be near the security of home as driving forces in consumer decisions.

We expect the same pattern in SEA, and we see domestic travel whether for business or leisure kickstarting the recovery for the hospitality sector in the region.

As economic activity resumes, we are starting to see an uptick in bookings from business travelers and also local tourists at a majority of our properties in countries where the isolation protocols have been lifted. During a recent long weekend in Vietnam, we saw a double digit increase in occupancy.

It will still take some time before we return to pre-covid levels. Unlike the bigger chains and network hotels who may be present in the major cities, OYO's presence extends beyond the main cities and to second and third tier towns and provinces across SEA, which adds to our appeal as the hotel of choice for business travelers and locals alike. With our network and reach, we expect the pace of recovery to be faster for us compared to hotels in the four to five-star category.

OYO CARE INITIATIVE

This was written by oyo staff during pandemic time. Here they had explained how they had tried their best to help people during their tough times. Now words are said by them.

We are cognizant of the aftermath caused by the COVID-19 pandemic and as a conscious hospitality chain taking several measures to help mitigate its effect. We value the immense contribution of our front line heroes who have been at the forefront fighting the war against this pandemic. On the occasion of Independence Day, we pledge to continue supporting the quarantine, self-isolation & accommodation requirements of such front-line workers and corporates under our 'OYO Care' initiative. We are happy to share that we have partnered with 24+ State Ministries, 50+ hospitals and local authorities and are offering some of our properties for pay per use quarantines, self-isolation facilities at affordable prices to minimize the possibility of infection and maximize social distancing and hygiene.

As part of the 'OYO Care' initiative, we are in touch with 50+ government and private hospitals to provide accommodation support to medical first responders at affordable prices. These efforts are in line with the advisories by WHO for doctors and paramedical staff treating COVID-19 patients to be isolated after their routine duties. Under the same initiative, we have already provided 100K room nights in the past four months. The hospitals which have been supported by OYO include – Safdarjung Hospital, Dr Ram Manohar Lohia Hospital and Sakra Hospital. Our long term rental business; OYO Life, is also working closely with multiple hospitals by extending support in offering long-term stays to nurses and healthcare professionals. We have also provided last-mile accommodation support to 500+ corporations including Ericsson, L&T, Omega Healthcare in July itself.

In the wake of the second wave of the pandemic, there is a dire need to build capacity and support the health care system with existing infrastructure. Extending its support to India's healthcare system and in the interest of the general public, we at OYO, have also rolled out a feature on the OYO app, wherein users can now book their quarantine stay through the app itself.

To support the nation's efforts to break the chain and flatten the curve of the virus, OYO Care tied up with several hospitals, ministries and government authorities to offer quarantine facilities for stranded tourists, frontliners, the medical community and asymptomatic patients. In light of the rising cases in the second wave of COVID-19, we will reinitiate the OYO Care initiative to further support the quarantine requirements of COVID-19 positive patients as well.

We, at OYO Care have tied up with 30+ hospitals, several government authorities and private sector companies to open its doors to dedicated properties across cities as self-isolation and quarantine centers for healthcare professionals, frontline workers and offer a safe stay for relatives of COVID-19 positive patients near hospitals and several others. Currently, it is also serving the accommodation requirements for the employees of local government bodies. We also stand ready to provide accommodation for post-travel isolation for tourists, and individuals traveling for emergencies, and other reasons.

To ensure the health and safety of its guests, employees, partners and vendors, we have implemented several precautionary and hygienic measures. Some of these include **Sanitized Stays, Sanitised Before Your Eyes, Contactless Check-ins, App and WhatsApp-based assistance with its chatbot – Yo! Chat**. Since its launch in October 2020, we have conducted 3.5 million safe check-ins with Sanitised Before Your Eyes.

TIME FOR BOUNCE BACK

This is how Oyo converted COVID's challenge into opportunity

The Covid-19 pandemic came out to be a bane for the whole world. For the hospitality industry's giant Oyo, it was the single biggest challenge it ever faced.

Hotel and homes provider Oyo rolled out tech-enabled improvements in several areas be it in a product, OTA operations, refund systems, research on partner and customer decisions, dashboards, or follow-ups.

"Our pricing algorithms are working to ensure optimum revenue. Through our AI and Machine Learning models, we've understood the guests' travel preferences and behaviors throughout the year,"

Anil Goel, Group Technology & Product Officer, Oyo, said

The pricing algorithm, which factors in historical behavior of the guests as well as a competitive data set at a city-level, enables Oyo to understand consumer elasticity and offer the best prices to its guests while keeping occupancies high for all hotel partners.

Several hotel partners in India, US and SEAME made use of this analysis and achieved 15-20% jump in conversion as compared to Oyo's competition, claims Goel.

Oyo is also leveraging artificial Intelligence to get calculated leads and help Demand Managers in contracting a building into an Oyo hotel within three meetings by helping with a checklist of things to look at, identify and determine decisions on.

"This is in stark comparison to the traditional methods where signing a building for a hotel can take months," said Goel.

Furthermore, real-time 24*7 chat assistant 'Yo! Help' has also been introduced. With the chat assistant, Oyo has been able to resolve queries across India within an Average Handling Time (ATH) of 01 minute as compared to a call center's ATH of 8-10 minutes.

As per Oyo's third annual travel index, Travelopedia 2020 -- a total of 24,07,992 sessions took place between guests and the automated bot.

Reducing costs with IT

To seamlessly onboard partners in today's world, Oyo has enabled a self onboarding tool for potential partners, a self-auditing tool for Go-live and a self-serve app for partners to answer questions around reconciliation to enable higher transparency.

"The pandemic brought the hospitality industry to a standstill. To ensure that we turn this challenge into an opportunity, we increased direct demand to the OYO app by upscaling it and driving more demand in web traffic, thereby minimizing our dependence on OTA," he said.

On the revenue front, a self-service tool for B2B customers and automated manual processes around content management, review management and OTA management were enabled. To enable remote working for the employees, tools were built to enhance remote operating capabilities and optimize use of infrastructure facilities and transportation.

Cloud-first approach

Since most of Oyo's tech stack was built with a 'cloud-first' principle, most of its internal and external workloads exist on the cloud.

"This not only gives us the agility to scale our offering across multiple availability zones in the cloud but also provides us the luxury to use out of the box offerings of our cloud partners to accelerate innovation," Goel said.

The hospitality company constantly evaluates managed vs self-managed offerings on the cloud, which keeps the cost and the speed of innovation balanced.

"It is really important for new-age companies to have a solid DevOps team which has experience in engaging with the cloud providers to run highly efficient and scalable offerings on the cloud. We at Oyo are lucky to have a well-experienced DevOps team with expertise on all major cloud providers across the world," he averred.

Marketing and Promotions

Social media marketing enabled OYO's customers to engage with the brand. OYO launched #CheckInForLove a week before Valentine's Day in 2020. The company reported a 284% increase in sentiment as the social media campaign rode on the popularity of cult art and pop culture. Bookings during the campaign period increased 90.57%.

As India initiated a staggered unlock approach, OYO rolled out 'Fir Badhega India' campaign. The campaign urged the Indians to move forward with hope and resilience. This was followed by a 'Road Trippin' campaign that urged customers to come to OYO properties. OYO unveiled the 'Contactless

Check-in' campaign across online and offline media channels. It depicted how check-in at OYO was completely contactless. Celebrity Sonu Sood was roped in as the brand ambassador and featured in the 'Sanitized Before Your Eyes' (SBYE) initiative. The tagline 'Pehle Spray Fir Stay' reinforced OYO's adherence to COVID-19 appropriate behavior. OYO unveiled the 'Long-term relationship with OYO' campaign. It had four digital films and its launch emerged from the insight that women played a key role in the travel related decision. OYO launched 5-day #OYOLove campaign. Unveiled during Valentine's week of 2021, the cricket-themed campaign engaged the target market and lent excitement to the employees as well as hotel owners. The customer engagement initiative led to an increase in walk-ins, revenue, as well as NPS (Saxena, 2021). OYO rolled out innovative sales promotion schemes in order to maintain cash inflows. OYO Wowcher and BOGO were two such products. Wowcher allowed users to redeem twice the value of payment made while Bogo allowed 100% flexibility and enabled users to plan future travels.

Flexible packages with the option to reschedule the event free of cost were given to the customers. Wedding solutions were devised for smaller gatherings.

INTERVIEW OF RITESH AGARWAL AFTER PANDEMIC

THE PANDEMIC IMPACT

Q- Tell us how the pandemic impacted your business, and the things you did to bring the graph back again into the positive.

I will break this answer up into two parts. First, the impact of Covid-19 and how we first responded and stabilized our ship, and second, how we are working towards resurgence and growing in the future. The pandemic impacted us for the first time in March and April 2020, when our gross margin in dollars fell over 66%. That was something that we'd built over a long period of time and that dropped substantially. Our perspective was that whenever there is an impact of such a crisis, there should be a simple way for everybody to understand how to deal with it. We thought the way to deal with the crisis was going to be care, cash, and evolution.

Let me start with cash. Within cash, our company worked on ensuring we speak to customers and owners so that we can protect and recover whatever revenue we can. So we learned that there were four or five types of customer trends that were going on. Staycations were growing. We doubled down and ensured that our entire marketing, products, and supply were designed towards staycations. The second is, we saw there was a rise in work-from-anywhere. We prepared work-from-anywhere to be our focused concept. We saw a big shift to online from offline, so we doubled down on digital-based reservations. We saw that value for money was critical. We saw healthcare and sanitation were critical, and we made sure we had [initiatives like] 'Sanitised Before Your Eyes', where people can see their rooms being sanitized before them. And recently, [we launched] VaccinAid, which are hotels where the entire staff has been vaccinated. And these hotels have seen much higher revenue. These are things we did to ensure the revenue was focused.

Q- OYO is now raising $600 million by way of a Term Loan B offering. What will you do with the money?

Our company already had a healthy balance sheet through the crisis. Our perspective was that we should try and bring institutional capital providers as partners in our business as we build it forward. As a part of that, we also chose to get rated by Moody's and Fitch. After our rating, we announced our intention to raise $600 million. The intention is to hold ourselves to higher levels of accountability and have slightly extra capital to have a fortress balance sheet around ourselves. There was some speculation about whether this was because of the impact of the second wave. I want to clarify that was not the reason. We went out to begin the rating process in January 2021, when India was at its best period.

On the [hotel] owners' side, it was very critical that we went back to them and ensured we used Covid-19 as a time to tell our partners that we would work together with them to come out of this crisis. We helped them with new kinds of products and software—lots of features were launched which either improved revenue or brought simplicity and lower costs of operations for them. Every week, I did a town hall with our hotel owners around the world to try and continuously improve things. So this was the first [aspect].

The second was to use technology to operate the business better. We made sure that today 85% of the customer service and 80%-plus of the merchant service are served through chat and chatbots. Customers and hotel owners like it because earlier they had to wait in a queue to get a service. Now they get it much quicker. Of course, we have to keep improving on it. So these kinds of efforts were taken, combined with our efforts to get whatever business we could. For example, over the past six-seven months, we have served over half a million nights in quarantine/ frontliners accommodation. This is just in India. We also had similar services in every country we operate.

BETWEEN THE LINES

(1) Pandemic shock: Covid-19 hit OYO Hotels & Homes hard in March-April 2020, when its gross margin in dollars fell over 66%. However, the measures it took worked, and the company (whose parent is called Oravel Stays Private Limited) says gross profits are back at more than 100% of pre-Covid-19 levels.

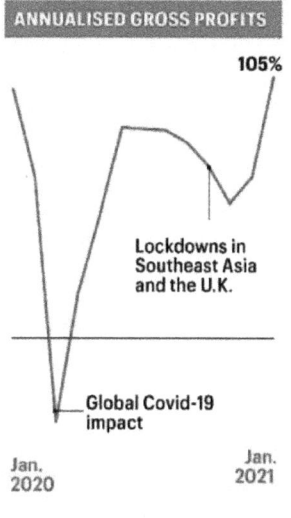

ANNUALISED GROSS PROFITS

105%

Lockdowns in Southeast Asia and the U.K.

Global Covid-19 impact

Jan. 2020 — Jan. 2021

Note: In $ mn, indexed to Jan'20 level
Source: OYO investor presentation

(2) Safety conscious: At properties which display the VaccinAid logo, OYO says that all staff have taken the first shot of the vaccine. Customers can also have their rooms sanitised in their presence.

(3) Global footprint: OYO today operates in 80 countries. According to its investor presentation, in January, India and Southeast Asia contributed 43.2% of its total revenue, Europe contributed 28.2%, and the rest of the international markets 28.6%.

(4) The app factor: According to App Annie Intelligence estimates, as of April 16, 2021, the OYO Rooms app was the third most downloaded app on iOS and Google Play combined, after Booking.com and Airbnb.

TOP TRAVEL APPS

1. **Booking.com**
2. **Airbnb**
3. **OYO Rooms**
4. **VRBO Vacation Rentals***
5. **Ctrip**

*from Expedia Inc. NOTE: Maps and navigation apps are excluded. Source: App Annie, OYO investor presentation

The third thing is making sure that there was care that we demonstrated. As the Covid-19 second wave hit, we saw that a lot of our employees were not able to take the time out to focus on things, not just at work but also not being able to spend time [on their own], with family, friends, etc. So we moved the company to a four-day week in order to make sure that people could make time for themselves. We also ensured that leaves were not ones that people needed to discuss; if you needed leave you just took it. We, unfortunately, lost four of our OYOpreneurs—fulltime and contracted employees. So we set up a bereavement policy for them. We've tried to do everything we can within our ability to try and make a difference in these times. But as a combination, this is what we did to deal with the crisis.

RIDING ON TECHNOLOGY

Q- How did you then focus on recovery?

We doubled down in terms of our product and engineering investments. I started spending 70%-plus of my time on engineering. We increased our engineering and product investments between 2019 and 2021 by 60%. And we are investing as we speak. We launched several market innovations. All of these were part of this rapid transformation into the future. A lot of this is in service and in ensuring that consumer demand comes [in]. Even on the merchant side, 30%-40% of the new hotels that are joining our platform are coming through our reseller network, where our hotel owners themselves recommend to other hotel owners to come and join the OYO platform. So our ability to be able to innovate with products has allowed us to make sure that we not just recovered from the pandemic but have also been able to get a substantial amount of growth, as well as the bottom line matrix, in the right trends.

Q- You had problems pre-pandemic too with some of your hotel owners who weren't happy with OYO. While you say you've taken steps to improve the experience for

them, how are you planning to recover from the hit the brand has taken as a result?

To begin with, I think our focus on making sure that our hotel owner experiences improve, and our customer experiences remain top-notch, is very critical. Within both these things, if I were to lay it out, there are a few reasons why our consumers and merchants have continued to appreciate us, and a few areas of improvement which we have used the last year almost as an opportunity to create an antidote— not just to the crisis but also with some of the improvements that were due anyway.

Let me start with the hotel owners. They like us typically for two to three critical reasons. The first is, we are able to give them improved business. The second is, our consumer app is the third most downloaded travel app in the world as per App Annie's recent trends. Our ability to give them software like Co-OYO and OYO OS allows them to operate their hotels better. That's why they like us.

" I started spending 70%-plus of my time on engineering. We increased our engineering and product investments between 2019 and 2021 by 60%. And we are investing as we speak."

- Ritesh Agarwal
(founder and CEO, of OYO Hotels & Homes)

In terms of areas of improvement, two things allowed us to improve our partner satisfaction rates. As a result, the number of complaints has rapidly reduced today and are limited mostly to a few situations from before the pandemic that we are still solving, and [in] that, [viewed in] compared to serving 190,000 merchants, we have come a long way. Within that, the first thing that has enabled us is a simple business model—where we give our software and charge a revenue share for it—which has allowed our hotel owners to have simpler visibility of our overall business.

Also, we are able to make sure that hotel owners do not lose their consumer focus. The second thing we have done is to concentrate on our technology and make sure that the earnings have been made simpler to understand by means of the OYO Secure programme we have set up with our hotel partners. We have ensured that the pricing has been improved by way of the tariff manager product, and the service speed has rapidly improved. Today we are able to use the 'help' section in our Co-OYO and OYO OS apps to give either instant- or less-than-15 minutes first response times which allows our merchants to have a happier experience than earlier, when they had to wait for someone to come to the hotel and support them.

I am happy to share that our partner satisfaction rates have gone up by 30 points. It's not to say we've done a great job. It's more to say this was due, and now we are excited about not just being where we are and being satisfied with being good. We want to be the best for our hotel partners, and every day my colleagues and I wake up and say what can we do better, while of course keeping consumers' interests and the right economics in mind.

DENMARK BUSINESS

OYO Rooms started their Danish adventure with the acquisition of the Danish holiday chains DanCenter and Danland in 2019. The new acquisition of Bornholmske Feriehuse underlines OYO's commitment to 'Invest in

Denmark' and to accelerating the growth of travel and tourism in the Danish market.

Invest in Denmark has assisted OYO in expanding their activities in Denmark, by being a part of the company's strategic planning process and by helping them connect with relevant local government stakeholders. Talking about India-Denmark Relations H.E. Freddy Svane, Danish Ambassador to India said,

"The relationship between India and Denmark has never been stronger. Tourism and culture plays an important role in building bridges between people and nations and I hope that this investment by OYO Rooms into the island of Bornholm will enable visitors to experience the strong focus on sustainable tourism in the region"

- H.E. Freddy Svane
(Denmark's Ambassador to India)

"Our guest nights have broken records in recent years, and the demand from foreign guests in holiday homes has been particularly high. The collaboration with OYO through DanCenter A/s therefore gives us the opportunity to keep up with demand, just as our homeowners also benefit from the many online portals that DanCenter collaborates with. The agreement may help our many holiday home owners achieve a higher rental percentage, while also contributing income and jobs to Bornholm."

- Rasmus Lund
(Director of Bornholmske Feriehuse)

"I feel elated as we welcome director Rasmus Lund and integrate Bornholmske Feriehuse under the brand OYO.

With increasing demand for holiday homes, Bornholm exhibits great potential for tourism in the coming years. We are happy to collaborate and work for the development of tourism in Bornholm and Denmark."

- Ritesh Agarwal
(Founder and CEO, OYO Rooms and Hotels)

MARRIAGE

(TIME FOR CELEBRATION)

Ritesh Agarwal, OYO Rooms' founder, and CEO married Geetansha Sood on March 7 , 2023. His wedding was followed by a grand reception at a five-star hotel in Delhi.

Whom invitation has been sent

OYO Founder Ritesh Agarwal and Geetansha Sood got married recently in a closed wedding ceremony. The function was joined by people like PayTM's Vijay Shekhar Sharma, Lenskar's Piyush Bansal and Softbank's Masayoshi Son. The couple had also invited President Draupadi Murmi and PM Modi on their wedding day and many other popular and famous personalities like them.

This image shows that Ritesh and his wife are inviting our honorable prime minister Shri shri narendra modi for their wedding.

Ritesh posted a picture after meeting with our honorable pm

riteshagar With the blessings of माननीय Pradhan Mantri @narendramodi ji, we are all set for a new beginning. Words cannot express the warmth with which he received us.

My mother, who is inspired by his vision for women empowerment & Geet, from Express(Uttar) Pradesh, were heartened to meet him. Thank you for sparing your valuable time & for your good wishes.

Ritesh Agarwal's wife, Geetansha Sood?

According to media reports, Geetansha is a native of Lucknow in Uttar Pradesh. However, this information has not been revealed by herself, her husband or her family.

DNA reported that Geetansha Sood is the director of Formation Ventures Limited, which is a private firm. The company is registered in Kanpur in its Registrar of Companies on August 22, 2020. Sood has paid Rs 1 lakh towards the company's shares. There are two other directors of this company, which are two and half years.

Ritesh and Geetansha

FATHERS DEATH (hard times)

Oyo Rooms founder Ritesh Agarwal's father Ramesh Agarwal died today after falling from the 20th floor of a Gurugram high-rise building. This comes days after Ritesh Agarwal's wedding.

In a statement, Ritesh Agarwal requested "everyone to respect our privacy in this time of grief".

"With a heavy heart, my family and I would like to share that our guiding light and strength, my father, Shri Ramesh Agarwal, passed away on 10 March. He lived a full life and inspired me and so many of us, every single day. His death is a tremendous loss for our family. My father's compassion and warmth saw us through our toughest times and carried us forward. His words will resonate deep in our hearts. We request everyone to respect our privacy in this time of grief," Ritesh Agarwal said.

The DCP, Gurugram East, said the police got information about the incident around 1 pm today. "The police were told Ramesh Agarwal fell from the 20th floor of the high-rise building DLF The Crest. He fell from his apartment's balcony and at the time of his death, his wife, son Ritesh Agarwal, and his (newly-wed) wife were at the apartment. No suicide note was found. There has been no complaint from the family over the circumstances of the death," he said.

Ritesh and his late father Shri Ramesh Agarwal

MEETING RISHI SUNAK

" It was wonderful to meet UK Prime Minister Rishi Sunak during the #UKIndia Week in London and discuss our collective vision to empower businesses across India and the UK. He truly understands the pivotal role that startups can play in creating more economic opportunities. We discussed OYO's investments in the UK, where we plan to add 50 new hotels this year.

Thank you, honorable sir, for your valuable time and encouragement. India and the UK are bound by strong ties of history and culture, and this relationship will be strengthened further by the proposed free-trade agreement. Here's to an exciting decade of growth, innovation, and collaboration ''

- Ritesh Agarwal tweeted

Rishi sunak and Ritesh

BECOMING FATHER (unforgettable moment)

Ritesh Agarwal, the CEO of OYO, shared the wonderful news on October 13, announcing his wife Geetansha Sood's pregnancy through a heartfelt social media post. In a beautiful note to wife, Ritesh shared their journey from " being children, to teenagers, to partners, to parents."

The billionaire, who tied the knot with Geetansha earlier this year 2023 , posted an endearing picture with her, expressing his excitement about embarking on the journey of parenthood together.

In a heartfelt message dedicated to his wife, Ritesh reminisced about their eleven-year journey, from his teenage years filled with dreams to the present, where they have experienced both joyous milestones and challenging moments side by side.

"I met Geet eleven years ago, when I was just a teenager chasing dreams, trying to convince my family that I wanted to build my own company from scratch. There was only one constant who was by my side through it all, and it was her.

The highs of happiness and milestones, the lows of pain and loss, we've been through so much together," wrote Ritesh.

"This year (2023) , we got married, which was one of the happiest moments of my life. And my family and I navigated through various highs and lows. Now, as Geet and I reflect on (and process) our transition from being children to teenagers, to partners, to parents, I couldn't be more excited. Our coming of age may have come and gone but I'm glad I got to share it all with you," he added.

Reflecting on their marriage this year as one of the happiest moments in his life, Ritesh shared his anticipation for the transition from being a couple to becoming parents, expressing his utmost excitement. He also playfully asked for suggestions regarding baby items like nappies, strollers, and toys from his social media followers, even welcoming innovative startup recommendations.

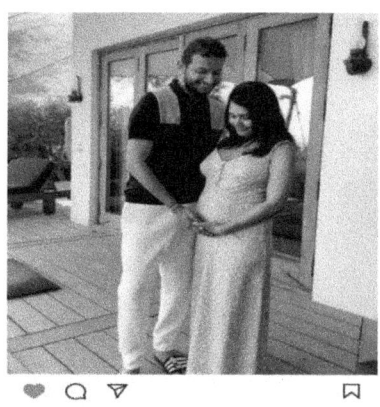

Ritesh and Geetansha sharing their happiest moment

YOUNGEST SHARK TANK OF INDIA

OYO Rooms founder Ritesh Agarwal has become the youngest Shark on the panel of Shark Tank India Season 3.

He will be joining the other Sharks - Aman Gupta (co-founder and CMO of boAt), Amit Jain (CEO and co-founder – CarDekho Group, InsuranceDekho.com), Anupam Mittal (founder and CEO of Shaadi.com – People Group), Namita Thapar (Executive Director of Emcure Pharmaceuticals), Vineeta Singh (Co-Founder and CEO of SUGAR Cosmetics) and Peyush Bansal (founder & CEO of Lenskart.com) - in the upcoming season.

Ritesh's debut video went viral after Sony Television announced his participation in Shark Tank India on social media.

SET India posted a video showing the Sharks sitting in their chairs, spinning around, and announcing the third season's newest Shark. The video was uploaded to the channel with the title "Shark Reveal! Welcoming our new Shark Ritesh Agarwal, Founder and CEO, of OYO Rooms, to Shark Tank India. Stay tuned for more exciting updates! #SharkTankIndia season 3 streaming soon on Sony LIV."

Ritesh post on becoming the youngest shark in India

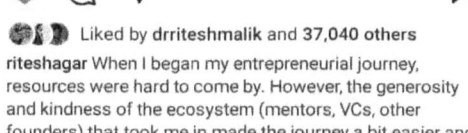

riteshagar When I began my entrepreneurial journey, resources were hard to come by. However, the generosity and kindness of the ecosystem (mentors, VCs, other founders) that took me in made the journey a bit easier and more fulfilling. To be able to replicate this has been a long-standing goal of mine. Whenever the opportunity presented itself, it made me extremely happy to connect with, mentor and back entrepreneurs at every stage of their own personal journeys.

I have extended my support to numerous startups, provided guidance to entrepreneurs within the @naropafellowship cohort, assisted small businesses across India, and whenever possible, I have wholeheartedly contributed to the community that stood beside me during my formative years.

SPECIAL MOMENT OF HIS LIFE

Ritesh Agarwal on Thursday (7th december 2023) announced that he and his wife Geetansha Sood have become parents to a baby boy. The announcement comes nearly two months after he revealed their pregnancy and nine months after their wedding.

"The miracle of life is breathtaking, and our hearts are forever changed. Meet our precious little one – Aryan," he wrote on X (formerly Twitter), sharing a glimpse of the newborn.

"The sleepless nights spent building Oyo were just a warm-up for the sleepless nights of parenthood, and yet, I've never been happier than I am at this very moment."

RITESH AGARWAL POST'S AFTER BECOMING THE FATHER OF ARYAN

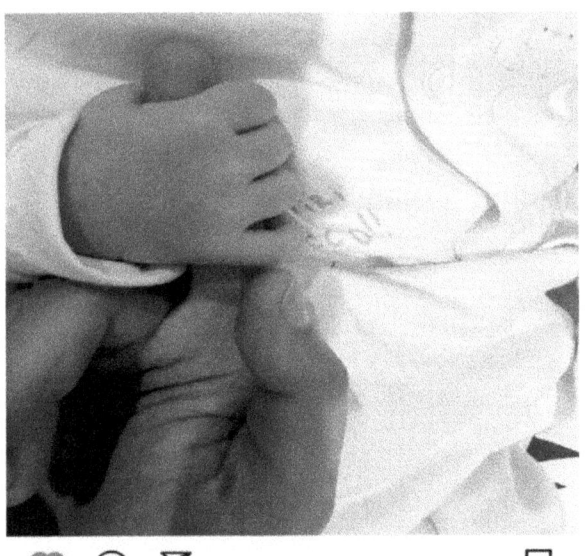

Liked by drriteshmalik and 15,488 others

riteshagar The miracle of life is breathtaking, and our hearts are forever changed. Meet our precious little one - Aryan. The sleepless nights spent building OYO were just a warm-up for the sleepless nights of parenthood, and yet, I've never been happier than I am at this very moment! Here's to us, my incredible wife Geet, the bundle of joy Aryan and to the new chapter we're writing together – filled with love, laughter, and the indescribable happiness that only a little one can bring. 💜

Ritesh plan's to Set Up 5 Healthcare Centres In Odisha By 2024

Ritesh announced the establishment of five healthcare centers in Odisha over the next year.the centers will be operated by the health-tech **startup** 'Last Mile Care', which already runs 11 health centers across India.

Ritesh said, "As we navigate the ever-evolving healthcare landscape, collaboration between healthcare providers, tech innovators, policymakers, and communities is paramount. By fostering an environment conducive to innovation and investing in initiatives such as these, we are doing our bit to ensure that quality medical services become accessible to everyone."

The company, in an official release, said it would provide free doctor consultations for the first three months and discounted treatment and medicine for everyone during the first six months. However, it has given no clarity on any charitable treatments after the first six months are over.

It is unclear whether the treatments or the medicines during the first three months will be free or discounted.

The company did not disclose the budget plan for setting up these five healthcare centers.

The centers will have a team of doctors with specialization in gynecology, eye diseases and heart diseases. A pharmacy will also be available to offer complete healthcare solutions to patients, the company claimed. The services include preventive care, diagnostic services, primary healthcare services, treatment for minor illnesses, professional consultation, referral services, affordable medication, and digital health record facilities.

The first center, the Ramesh and Bela Agarwal Healthcare Center, was inaugurated by Jagannath Saraka, the state minister for SC & ST Development, Minorities and Backward Class Welfare and Law. The center has been named in honor of Ritesh Agarwal's parents, the late Ramesh Agarwal and Bela Agarwal.

"The strategic placement of these centers aims to cover regions with limited access to healthcare facilities, thereby bridging the gap between healthcare services and marginalized populations," the company stated.

RITESH POST AFTER OPENING

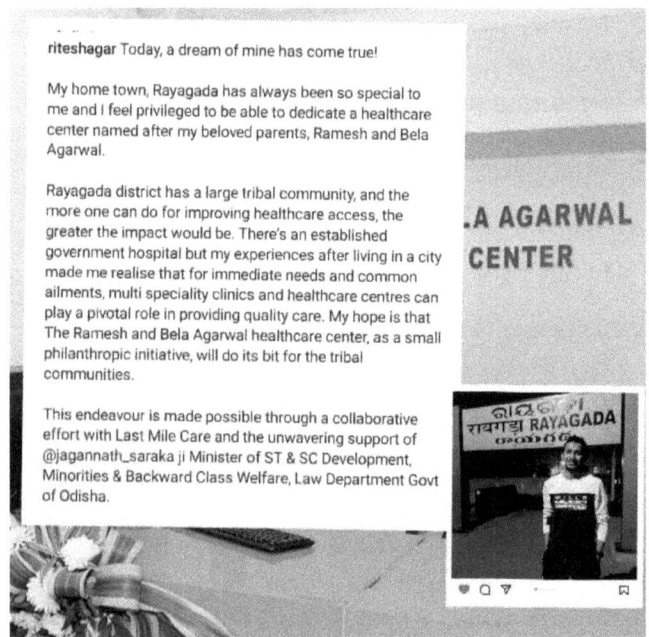

WHAT YOU HAVE LEARNT NOW, MAKE SOME NOTES SO THAT YOU CANNOT FORGET

CHAPTER 7
ALLEGATIONS AND CONTROVERSIES

"WHEN YOU FEEL THE ENTIRE WORLD IS AGAINST YOU, THERE IS STILL A LITTLE VOICE IN THE BACK OF YOUR HEAD THAT KEEPS SAYING... "YOU CAN DO IT, I KNOW YOU CAN!"

THAT IS BECAUSE YOU CAN"

1st ALLEGATION

He had some harsh times with his co-founders and employees at Oravel. Some even say that Ritesh is an outright liar and that he cannot code. Kunal Pandya of NCrypted Technologies (a Gujarat-based technology firm) said that he had licensed his vacation rental portal 'BistroStays' to Ritesh in return for some shares, something which never happened.

Detail explanation of controversy

Kunal Pandya, CEO of Gujarat-based NCrypted, which calls itself a startup enabler, says his company had licensed its vacation rental product Bistro Stays to the founder when Oyo Rooms was called Oravel. Pandya recently called Agarwal out on Twitter for his alleged coding skills, as reported by a leading national newspaper.

This Letter was sent by kunal pandya to NDTV for his side of the story. What follows is the letter Pandya sent.

The media is giving too much attention and hype to Ritesh Agarwal, founder of Oyo Rooms, and seems to be posting whatever he has to share. What's surprising is that Ritesh is trying to present himself as a 'coder' in front of the media - surprising because Oyo's parent company Oravel has been our NCrypted's client, and we knew Ritesh from before he was famous.

The truth is that the early days of Oravel and Oyo were built on a foundation of lies and Ritesh seems to have faked almost everything that stands as his founding pillars, from his education to funding rounds.

In the early days, I was a partner to Ritesh when he was new to the industry, and can personally comment on some of the myths behind the Oyo story.

Let me tell you one thing straight away - the guy is an outright liar. He knows no coding and has faked almost every credential prior to his funding rounds. I have not been in contact with him since Oyo's second round of VC funding with Sequoia in early 2015, and can't comment if he learned some kind of coding afterwards, but much of what had to happen happened already by then.

His age has certainly played a factor behind much of this hype and people got curious as to how a 21 year old can build such a website and a business around it. This is the true story of how he got started, and how NCrypted played a major role in building his career.

Chapter 1 - Ritesh Agarwal meets Kunal Pandya of NCrypted to develop his website

Ritesh contacted us in June 2012 to enquire about our vacation rental product BistroStays. Apart from the domain license, he required many customisations as well. This was before Oyo Rooms was launched, and Ritesh had just gotten started with Oravel, which had a couple of static pages and practically no traffic.

At this time, the business did not have any VC or angel funding at all. Ritesh hadn't gone for the much hyped Peter Thiel fellowship yet, and he hadn't joined Venture Nursery yet.

According to him, he 'tried' to attend college for a day, but the reality was he was just a 12th grader who knew some basics about websites and was very enthusiastic about the new dotcom boom in India.

Our job was simple just like any other software vendor - irrespective of who you are and what you do, if you want to buy our products and services, then we would be happy to serve.

Ritesh didn't know anything about coding; he just knew that he wanted to quickly create an Airbnb clone and get a couple of million dollars of funding. To do this, he needed our code- BistroStays lets you start your own vacation/ apartment rental website - without needing to know anything about coding. It is a bundled Web product and you don't require any programming knowledge to start and operate it.

Unfortunately, we soon found out that Ritesh and his company Oravel Stays didn't have the money to pay us. For months, we went to him with bills but didn't get any payment after the first upfront payment was made to start the project.

Ritesh desperately wanted to launch the site on the new product and kept on promising me personally that he would pay soon. Trust is a major factor in our industry, so we went ahead, deployed the product and activated the license file.

Here is how the site looked in January 2012 before it was deployed on our product. And here is a screenshot of the site taken in December 2012 after the site started running on our product. BistroStays was powering the site till mid-2013, when we had to withdraw and cancel the license due to payment issues.

The software allowed Ritesh to start listing sellers and buyers as they could sign up themselves. With the advanced admin panel back-end system, it was now possible for them to monitor and keep a track of what's happening with every single module that is in transition.

The SEO-friendly front-end helped as they started seeing some organic traffic on the site on their Delhi NCR property listings.

<u>Chapter 2</u> - Ritesh offers equity partnership to us since he couldn't pay in cash

Since we refused to continue working unless all outstanding dues were settled, Ritesh offered around 1.5 to 2 percent equity in Oravel Stays to me along with half payment settlement as per the dues. He shared his bank balance screenshot which had less than Rs. 50,000, and I already started to feel cheated." If you don't have money, why request such heavy customisations and force us to launch the site," I asked to myself.

Eventually, we decided that he was just a 21-year-old in over his head, and didn't think that he would be intentionally cheating us. And so we chose to believe him, because I rather wanted to back him. We are a startup enabler and all our products are targeted for startups and small to medium scale businesses. Their success is our success.

In July 2012, we worked out a deal for stock and cash wherein Oravel Stays will issue about 420 fresh shares to us, plus cash, and we continue the relationship. The papers were not yet signed as Ritesh insisted that we do so next month, just before getting funded.

Somewhere around in August, after the beta site was launched on our product, Ritesh told me that Venture Nursery has made the investment. This was a surprise to me, as Ritesh had still not signed our agreement, and now our money and our shares were at stake.

Ritesh had said Venture Nursery would invest somewhere between Rs. 50 to Rs. 75 lakhs but he then shared a picture of the cheque from Venture Nursery of just Rs. 5 lakhs. This was less than the dues he already owed us, and I started losing trust.

Apoorv Sharma, who was Executive VP of Venture Nursery at that time, called me to understand how the product works. Ritesh acknowledged this in an email exchange with Apoorv and me, writing that NCrypted has been a huge support in building Oravel's next high quality site and support.

So, Ritesh got the beta site live running on our product, and showcased that to Venture Nursery. Venture Nursery now got interested and enrolled him into its accelerator program, with a promise of Rs. 5 lakh investment.

Chapter 3 - Parting ways

With our product in the back-end, Oravel was shaping up fine. We were yet to get paid but kept working and trusting

Ritesh. We had two options - either quit or keep working, and we thought that if we quit, we would never recover the money he owed us.

So it seemed to be in the best of our own interest, at that time, to see to it that his website shapes up well and gets funded, so that we can get paid and have some real worth to our 'promised' equity.

Our accounts team meanwhile kept sending invoices to Ritesh and he continued delaying. I personally asked Ritesh to send us post dated cheques as security, until we have the agreement signed. Many of his cheques had already bounced by this time.

Ritesh slowly stopped updating me on funding rounds and his experience with VentureNursery; and our team, as per our commitment, continued working on his product.

Somewhere around in February 2013, Ritesh hired developers to work on Oravel.com. They took their own sweet time to learn the system.

Meanwhile Ritesh had our copyright notice removed from the site footer and this is how we got to know that he has started working with somebody else despite having all these promises of equity plus cash.

It was time that we had to part ways. I asked him to discontinue using the product as we will withdraw the license because of overdue accounting for more than six months. At the time, Ritesh continued to insist on an equity partnership.

Chapter 4 - The Thiel Fellowship

When Ritesh was still struggling with the new site development after we removed our product, luck came to his side.

Somewhere during March end 2013, Ritesh got the big news - he was selected as the first Indian to receive Thiel Fellowship. According to the Mint article, Ritesh wrote to his newly hired freelancers, "One thing is pretty urgent -Let's make the earlier code and database we had on the live site... Until then we can't afford to have the 20 under-20 guys take a note of us not having a real product... we can use the situation to our advantage in the manner of launching the day we have the final conference (13th)."

This archive of Oravel.com taken on April 23, 2013 shows they were present in more than 60 cities in India and had properties in Singapore as well. Some of the city names are incorrect and the site is entirely static with no real back-end present. Any experienced coder should have recognised this, but that's not what happened.

Instead, they bought the story and Ritesh got lucky yet again. He not only received a $100,000 scholarship from the Thiel Foundation, but got a big Silicon Valley name backing his company.

In May, Venture Nursery arranged for a PR agency for press interviews on the Thiel fellowship. The rest of the story is published in Mint. Ritesh continued his saga of faking and screwing relationships once he got what he wanted from it after this as well.

In March 2013, Oravel finally discontinued using our product after a series of emailed requests. Ritesh refused to pay part of the remaining dues and argued that since Oravel was no longer using the product, it wouldn't pay for the product at all. Our legal team was planning to file a case but I didn't want to focus on this dead client, so I said that we will accept the remaining dues and preferred to focus on our own business.

While this was happening, Ritesh got the Thiel scholarship of $100,000 (approximately Rs. 66 lakh), and a couple of rounds of angel and VC funding, but he kept us in the dark, instead of paying the money he owed quickly.

I later learned that Venture Nursery and some other angel investors had put in Rs 30 lakh into Oravel after the initial Rs. 5 lakh, probably after the launch of the website running on our product. Ritesh never shared this with me, as otherwise he would have had to pay the dues and sign the stocks deal which he had promised.

During all this, Venture Nursery kept investing in media and PR, and Ritesh was noticed by the world, pitched as a 21-year-old coder with an angel backed venture, seeking more VC funding as the business is now ready to expand. Except of course, none of this was really true.

Chapter 5 - What comes next?

Guys like Rahul Yadav, the ex-CEO and founder of Housing.com, and Ritesh Agarwal of Oyo Rooms, are ruining the Indian startup ecosystem.

They are presenting themselves as India's Steve Jobs, projecting themselves as 'products guys' and if you read any media interviews of these guys, they constantly try to project themselves as big thinkers and innovators.

But when you look at it, what innovation has Oyo Rooms actually done? This entire idea is running behind the logic of launching an Airbnb clone in India, and later pivoting to an Uber type of business model.

Now, of course, you have to implement this in a new market and India brings its own set of hurdles, so hard work is accepted from that point of view. The problem rather is when these guys project themselves as so-called 'innovators'. And, hell, Ritesh went ahead and called all of his competition imitators and copycats?

Surprisingly, Softbank is a common large investor in both Housing and Oyo Rooms; both startups founded by big-mouthed 'visionaries'.

But the Indian audience and Internet users at large are not stupid. They don't want startup heroes. They simply want a solid product to solve their real life problems. If these guys can do that well while not trying to burn easy VC money, they will have a better chance. But that doesn't seem to be happening as Oyo Rooms' business model requires them to burn cash heavily, not just on operations and human resources, but on partner hotel retainers as well.

Hotels I've spoken to tell me that Oyo has to buy out a specific quota of rooms with partners on a monthly basis, whether or not they are able to re-sell them. That's why Oyo is able to offer hotels for Rs. 999 even though the hotel charges Rs. 2,000 if you go directly. Now you know where the $125 million funding is going.

For now, it benefits the hotels and the travelers, but there are problems that will certainly occur down the road. HomeJoy.com, a US based Uber-for-X startup faced this tough question after three years of its inception and had to shut down. Oyo is moving in the same direction right now.

Ritesh might have gotten lucky and was able to get funding rounds by selling fake numbers, but the end consumer is not stupid. They don't want to use Oyo just because it was built by a 21-year-old. They want to use it because they find something dirt cheap and too good to be true. The billion dollar question is - when the party ends and VC money dries up, how will Oyo be able to provide dirt cheap rates ?

DISCLAIMER: All the information of this letter was provided by the author of this letter who is kunal pandya i am not taking any responsibility of this letters accuracy or completeness.

2nd ALLEGATION

In September 2019, Bengaluru Police booked Ritesh and two of his representatives for cheating and criminal breach of trust following a businessman's complaint. In his complaint, Natarajan V R S, an ex- serviceman, stated that he runs the Rajguru Shelter Hotels in BEML Layout in Whitefield. He entered into an agreement with Ritesh Agarwal in June 2017, where Oyo would give them reservations and take 20% of the share and give him 80%, but Agarwal and his representatives had taken 80% of the share instead of 20%. He accused Ritesh and his representatives of cheating him of more than Rs. 1 Crore. The Whitefield Police booked Ritesh and his representatives under IPC Section 406 (criminal breach of trust) and 420 (cheating).

The Case Against OYO CEO Ritesh Agarwal

Natarajan, who runs the Rajguru Shelter Hotels in BEML Layout in Whitefield, said he entered into an agreement with Ritesh Agarwal in June 2017, where OYO would give them reservations and take 20% of the share and give him 80%. However, he alleges that Agarwal and his representatives in Bengaluru had taken 80% of the share instead of 20%.

He accused the trio of cheating him of more than INR 1 Cr. The Whitefield police booked the trio, including Agarwal, under IPC Section 406 (criminal breach of trust) and 420 (cheating). The chief inspector of Whitefield police station Narendra Kumar reportedly said that an investigation in the matter is being carried out. Also, Natarajan said that many hotels in Bengaluru had similar problems with OYO.

An OYO spokesperson told Inc42, "OYO Hotels & Homes has always maintained the highest level of integrity, transparency and commitment to its asset owners. We at all times follow the laws of the land and operate keeping in mind the best interests of our asset owners, customers and employees. This matter is currently sub judice, and we are not at the liberty of commenting on specifics. Having said that, we strongly refute the claims made in the complaint that has been wrongfully filed against our Founder and two other office bearers, basis false claims and exaggeration on a regular commercial dispute."

Our lawyers are looking into the matter and will be taking strong legal action as these claims are incorrect and defamatory in nature. We respect the law of the land and believe it will do the right justice.

3rd ALLEGATION

On 14 September 2020, the Mohali Police registered a case of "fraud and criminal conspiracy" against Ritesh Agarwal on the complaint of a Chandigarh businessman. In his complaint, the victim alleged that Ritesh and his team cheated him out of a business agreement illegally and with criminal intent.

The founder and CEO of Oyo Hotels and Homes Pvt Ltd (OHHPL), the country's well-known hotel chain, is in the dock as the Mohali police have registered a case of fraud and criminal conspiracy against him on the complaint of a Chandigarh-based businessman.

An FIR has been registered against Ritesh Aggarwal, founder, Oyo Hotels, and Sandeep Lodha, CEO of the OHHPL's brand Weddingz.in, on the complaint of Vikas Gupta.

VIKAS GUPTA, COMPLAINT

Despite terminating the agreement in a one-sided way and in a manner which smacks of 'criminal intent', my marriage palace's name is still being used and innocent people are being cheated in terms of money. There is proof that weddings have been booked till December 2020 and I am being made a scapegoat in the modus operandi.

The victim, in his complaint to the SSP, had alleged that the company's top management abruptly wriggled out of a business agreement illegally and with criminal intent. The SSP marked the complaint to the SP (Rural), Mohali, who, after conducting a thorough investigation, recommended registration of an FIR against the suspects.

Vikas Gupta said an agreement was signed between his company Vikas Mineral Foods Pvt Limited under which he also operated Banquet Hall Casa Villaz at Ramgarh-Mubarakpur road, Dera Bassi, Mohali, and Oravel Stays Pvt Ltd (OSPL). He said in June 2019, he came in contact with Virender Pal Bhasin, head, OHHPL, Chandigarh, who showed interest in his banquet hall. He said an agreement was signed, according to which the Weddingz.in team would handle the business and pay them a fixed amount every month in return.

Gupta said all documents and NOCs asked by the OHHPL to run his banquet hall were submitted and the top management, including the finance and legal teams, of Oyo was satisfied. Everything was running smoothly until the Covid outbreak restrictions were imposed on gathering in marriages and events, he added.

He alleged, "Fearing losses, the OHHPL hatched a conspiracy and against the terms of the signed agreement, sent him a notice on March 16 this year to again submit NOCs and other documents. They gave me a 15 days notice period, whereas according to the agreement, 60 days is the notice time to be given in case any party wants to break the agreement if any breach happens."

He said later another notice asking him to pay over Rs5 crore (approximately) penalty was sent to him, as part of a criminal conspiracy to make huge and easy money through pressure tactics. He said both notices sent to him were unsigned, so these had no legal sanctity.

4TH ALLEGATION

OYO Rooms has started an internal probe after Noida police arrested two people who allegedly put a hidden camera in a hotel room and filmed a couple.

The two accused had booked the same room in the Phase 3 police station area last month where they placed a hidden camera before checking out.

After a week, they booked the same room and took the camera out which had recorded the couple in intimate condition, officials said. Additional DCP (Central Noida) Saad Miyan Khan said the duo had made extortion attempts with the couple threatening to release their video online. While accused Vishnu Singh and Abdul Wahab were held, police also questioned the hotel staff over the incident but so far their role has not been found.

"The hotel and its staff were not found involved in the incident so far. The accused duo had stayed in the hotel in the past also and the police are contacting the guests who have stayed there in the recent past to confirm if anyone else also got an extortion call," ADCP Khan told PTI.

Meanwhile, there was no official comment from OYO over the episode but people associated with the company said they were internally probing the matter. "OYO does not operate any hotels or guest houses it only lists verified properties on its platform and provides IT-based support to them," a source told PTI

Police said an FIR has been lodged under IPC Sections 420,386,506,467, 468, 471, and 120B and further investigation is underway.

5TH ALLEGATION

FIR Against Founder Ritesh Agarwal In Bengaluru But OYO Refutes Charges

On Monday (4 November 2019), a Bengaluru hotelier filed a first information report (FIR) at the Ulsoor police station in Bengaluru against OYO founder and group CEO Ritesh Agarwal as well as others in the company. The complainant has alleged "criminal breach of trust", "cheating", "criminal conspiracy", "abetment", and "computer-related offenses" under Section 107, 120B, 405, 420 Of The Indian Penal Code 1860 and Section 66 of the Information and Technology Act, 2000 read with Section 156 of the Code of Criminal Procedure.

The case has been filed against Rohit Srivatsava, head of southern India for OYO, Madhvendra Kumar, head, of business development; Gourab De, head, of business development and in charge of property; Prateek Agarwal, finance, OYO and Manjeet Singh, finance, OYO and Mrinmoy Chakraborty, business development manager at OYO.

Roxel inn statement on filing this case

Elister Fernandez, CEO of Roxel Inn said that OYO hasn't paid them assured benchmark revenue of INR 7 Lakh each month, as signed under contract on May 23, 2019. Fernandez alleged that OYO has created multiple non-existent room bookings which it marked under no-show and cancellations.

Oyo statement on this allegation

an OYO spokesperson refuted "the claims made in the complaint that has been wrongfully filed against our founder and six other office bearers, based on false allegations and exaggeration on a regular commercial dispute." The police summoned the alleged accused to meet the investigating officer on November 7.

Why did Roxel Inn Filed AN FIR Against OYO ?

In its complaint, Fernandez has alleged that, "It is brought to notice that in the month of June, with an intention to cheat and cause wrongful loss, OYO and its team has created bogus bookings in various names to the property."

"However, none of this was forthcoming on paper or in reality and hence my company immediately correspond via email stating the details of the No-show and Cancellations of the bogus bookings made on the OYO platform and further requested to OYO and its team to adjust an amount of INR 7098/- for willful and negligent act of OYO and its team," he added.

> Sub-Inspector Of Police,
> Halasuru Police Station,
> Halasuru, Bangalore City.
>
> Date : 04-11-2019
>
> **POLICE NOTICE**
>
> (u/s 41(1) CRPC)
>
> This is to inform you that on 02-11-2019 one Shri Betz Fernandez appear to the police station, and lodged a complaint aginst 1) Ritesh Agarwal 2) Rohit Srivatsava 3) Madhvendra Kumar 4) Gourab De 5) Prateek Agarwal 6) Manjeeth Singh 7) Mrimony Chakraborty in Halasuru Police Station. Hence a Case is registered Vide Cr.No. 348/2019 u/s 406, 420, 120(B) r/w 34 IPC. So you are hereby directed to appear before the undersign Investigation Officer on 07-11-2019 at about 11-00 AM without fail, for enquiry.
>
> Sub Inspector of Police
> Halasuru Police Station
> Bangalore City
>
> To,
>
> 1) Ritesh Agarwal
>   CEO , OYO
> 2) Rohit Srivatsava
>   Head of South, OYO
> 3) Madhvendra Kumar
>   Head Business Development, OYO
> 4) Gourab De
>   Head Business Development, OYO
>   & Incharge of Property, OYO
> 5) Prateek Agarwal
>   Finance , OYO
> 6) Manjeeth Singh
>   Finance , OYO
> 7) Mrimony Chakraborty
>   Finance , OYO

41(1) CRPC NOTICE

ABOUT THIS NOTICE

As you can see in the above picture. This notice was issued by the police sub inspector of Halasuru police station of bangalore city. Let me give you some information about this notice although I am not an advocate / lawyer. I have taken help from my friend Rishabh who has a deep knowledge about this.

Let's talk about IPCs

- 406 = Taking money and not giving it back
- 420 = To cheat
- 120 (B) = The one who commits a crime and the one who stands with him are also guilty

Now let's talk about the notice

41 (A) notice of appearance before a police officer. In all cases where the arrest of a person is not required under the provisions sub section one of section 41 issue a notice directing the person against whom a reasonable complaint has been made or credible information has been received.

<u>6TH ALLEGATION</u>

OYO faced backlash from 10,000 hotel owners in India. According to them, OYO takes up half or more of the revenues through fees that are not disclosed at the time when the hotels join OYO.

India's Oyo Hotels and Homes shot out of nowhere to become one of the world's largest hotel chains with a simple promise of "hassle-free" online booking, transparent pricing and cheerful lodging.

But as the Softbank-backed startup pushes toward profitability, an increasing number of Indian hotel operators who have partnered with it are complaining about being blindsided by fee increases.

The backlash against Oyo - while limited to a small share of the more than 10,000 hotel owners in India who work with it - comes at a crucial time for an emerging-market unicorn valued at $10 billion and its major investor.

Softbank, which has invested nearly $1 billion in Oyo, through its Vision Fund, is struggling to raise funding for a second investment fund in the wake of the failed offering of office-rental company WeWork and amid questions about the path to profitability of other marquee investments like Uber. Oyo has not yet turned a profit.

In the background of the discontent is the disruption Oyo has brought to India's lodging market - often to the delight of India's middle-class travelers and to the dismay of hotel owners who have seen room rates driven down at a time when economic growth has slowed.

Oyo charges hotels a roughly 20% franchise fee on room revenues when hotels join its network, but some Indian hotel operators say the startup often ends up taking half or more of revenues through fees that were not initially disclosed.

A group representing hotel operators in Bengaluru called for a criminal probe into Oyo last month, saying the company was withholding money because of unfair fee increases.

Two hoteliers in the southern state of Karnataka filed separate police complaints last month accusing Oyo of deceitfully increasing commissions, and accusing Oyo's 25-year-old founder and CEO Ritesh Agarwal of fraud.

Agarwal successfully appealed to the Karnataka High Court for a stay order on one case in Bengaluru, the court website shows, and a police official said the order barred police from investigating.

In the other complaint, in the town of Chikkamagaluru, police are investigating, an official there said.

Oyo has denied the allegations and said Agarwal declined comment on the legal complaint. The company said it operates with a high level of "integrity, transparency and commitment" with its partners.

Agarwal said hotel operators who have raised complaints represent a tiny fraction of Oyo's network and were seeking to drive prices higher at the expense of consumers.

"On an annual basis, Oyo is able to retain 99% of its asset owners. If, for instance, people were unhappy, our retention rate would have been lower," he told Reuters.

Softbank, which owns a roughly 45% stake in Oyo, declined to comment.

'PLATFORM FEE' AND 'VISIBILITY BOOST'

Oyo says it is in constant contact with its hotel partners. "We have always disclosed any changes applicable to contracts with asset owners," Oyo said in a statement.

For their part, owners and managers say Oyo has introduced fees - including a "platform fee" and a fee for a "visibility boost" - which they only discovered in monthly statements.

Reuters interviews with 22 hotel owners and managers who run hotels under the Oyo brand in 10 Indian cities suggest the discontent has grown since late last year.

Several hotel groups have organized protests. Amitabh Mohapatra, head of one such group in northern India, says over 300 hotels have quit Oyo's India network this year, while Kunal Rajpara, who heads another group in western India, said a few dozen hoteliers from Ahmedabad ditched Oyo last month.

"The situation with Oyo has gone from bad to worse," said P.C. Rao, president of the Bruhat Bangalore Hotels Association. "We want to make sure the business of small hoteliers isn't hurt."

Some hotel operators say Oyo continued to list their properties on its mobile app with a "sold out" banner after they asked Oyo to sever ties.

Three hotel operators in Ahmedabad said they had emailed Oyo representatives on Sept. 23, asking to be removed from the platform but received no response. Reuters found all their properties still listed on Oyo's app with "sold out" messages even though the hotels had rooms available.

Oyo says once a hotel has served a 30-day notice period and accounts are settled, the property is typically delisted within 72 hours. It tags all properties serving their notice period that may deny check-ins to customers as "sold out", the company said.

'IT ISN'T SOMETHING OYO CAN IGNORE'

Founded in 2013, Oyo started by aggregating bookings for India's budget hotels, promising a standard of service in a market where that was more often the exception. Oyo has expanded to China, Europe and the United States, calling itself the world's fastest growing hotel chain.

Many hotel owners in India were upbeat when Oyo gave properties in smaller cities visibility but began to raise concerns when profits failed to improve, said Darshini Kansara, a hospitality industry analyst at CARE Ratings in Mumbai.

"It isn't something Oyo can ignore as they look to capture more market share."

Based in Gurugram, near New Delhi, Oyo signs up hotels as franchisees by rebranding them and upgrading amenities and then charges fees from the owners.

Oyo says hotels are updated on any new contract terms on a tablet-device at the hotel that Oyo provides to manage bookings.

But some hotel owners say the devices are operated by junior staff, leaving them in the dark until fees have been charged. Ashraf Ali, a hotelier in Mumbai, said a notification offering new terms would keep showing up on the tablets until the hotel employee hit accept.

Bengaluru hotelier Vikrant Singh says his 50-room hotel swung from making monthly profits of nearly $7,000 in late 2016 to a loss of more than $2,000 this January. He blames Oyo for the reversal.

"Our profits went down due to the high commissions Oyo was charging," said Singh, who withdrew his hotel from Oyo in March.

7th ALLEGATION

Allegations of cheating by Oyo's co-founder

Agarwal is accused of cheating Oyo's co-founder, Manish Sinha, during the early period of the company.

8TH ALLEGATION

Zostel's allegations against IPO

The DRHP is replete with material omissions and blatant misstatements, intended to mislead the public to invest in Oravel's shares without an appreciation of the risks involved, Zostel had stated

OYO's parent firm Oravel Stays has refuted all 'allegations' made by Zostel Hospitality, which had requested the markets regulator Sebi to reject the draft red herring prospectus filed by OYO for its initial public offering.

In a letter to the Securities and Exchange Board of India on October 11, 2021, Zostel had said "the IPO is non-maintainable as Oravel's capital structure is not final" and accordingly "Oravel's filing of the DRHP (Draft Red Herring Prospectus) in the circumstances, is illegal..."

The DRHP is replete with material omissions and blatant misstatements, intended to mislead the public to invest in Oravel's shares without an appreciation of the risks involved, it had added.

In a letter to Zostel, accessed by PTI, OYO said, "...we deny in toto all the allegations leveled by you against us in the Complaint. The Complaint is replete with patently false statements and self-serving half-truths, and is a deplorable attempt to adversely impact the proposed Offer and coerce the Company into granting Zostel's shareholders an entitlement to shareholding in the company that they failed to obtain in the arbitration proceedings between Zostel, its founders and shareholders and the company and the arbitral award dated March 6, 2021, issued by the sole arbitrator, Justice AM Ahmadi (Retd.)".

The company has made adequate disclosures required under the applicable law in the DRHP filed with Sebi. No reasons or grounds, whatsoever, have been made out by you, warranting consideration of rejection of the DRHP or suspension of the proposed offer, it added.

"The capital structure of the Company is firm and accurately reflected in the DRHP. As on date, there are no shares due to be issued to Zostel's shareholders as the Award does not direct issuance of the Company's shares to the shareholders of Zostel," the letter said.

All outstanding litigation required to be disclosed in accordance with the ICDR Regulations and the materiality policy adopted by the board of directors of the company in relation to outstanding litigation, involving the company, its subsidiaries, its promoters and its directors have been disclosed in the DRHP, it added.

Further, this matter has been disclosed in the section "Outstanding Litigation and Material Developments - Litigation involving our Company - Material litigation against our Company" of the DRHP. A risk factor in relation to the matter has also been disclosed in the DRHP, OYO said.

"...the DRHP contains adequate disclosures of all pending litigations, in compliance with the disclosure obligations under the ICDR Regulations," it added.

The DRHP or the proposed offer do not infringe upon or violate the terms of the Award or any judicial or quasi-judicial pronouncements. Adequate information and disclosures have been provided in the DRHP for the potential investors to make an informed decision in respect of investment in the equity shares and the proposed offer, OYO said.

Comments from Zostel Hospitality Pvt Ltd could not be obtained at the time of filing the story.

ZO-ZOSTEL AND OYO ROOMS FULL CONTROVERSIES

OYO and Zo Rooms have been in a legal tussle for over three years now.

The dispute was over the merger between OYO and Zo Hostels, where the latter said it was denied its 7% shareholding in Oravel Stays, the parent company of OYO.

The tribunal said that Zo Rooms' parent Zostel Hospitality was entitled to claim relief and costs in the case, but acknowledged that definitive agreements weren't executed.

After a three-year long battle, the legal verdict on OYO Hotels and Homes and Zo Hostels is out, but both companies continue to sing their own tunes. The dispute was over the merger between OYO and Zo Hostels, where the latter said it was denied its 7% shareholding in Oravel Stays Pvt. Ltd, the parent company of the Ritesh Agarwal-led OYO.

The Arbitral Tribunal comprising former Chief Justice of India AM Ahmadi said that Zo Rooms' parent Zostel Hospitality Pvt. Ltd was entitled to claim relief and costs in the case, but acknowledged that definitive agreements of the deal weren't executed.

Two sides of the same coin

Zo Rooms, which was a hotel aggregator founded by Zostel founders, claimed victory in the case saying that the agreement between OYO and Zo was binding. "We welcome the judgement by the hon'ble tribunal. Beyond the monetary compensation, it was a fight for our rights and reputation. We are extremely relieved with the judgement that the arbitral tribunal has pronounced after diligently evaluating the merits and evidence produced by us over the last 3 years," said Paavan Nanda, co-founder of Zostel, who led the process, in a statement. Nanda is also the co-founder of gaming platform WinZO.

As per Zo, OYO now has to compensate the stakeholders of Zo for their 7% shares. "If the order from the arbitrator is to be given effect, allotment of 7% to ZO Rooms' shareholders will make this outcome the biggest exit in the Indian startup ecosystem, surpassing the Snapdeal-Freecharge Deal of $400 Million back in 2015," said Zo in a statement.

However, OYO refuted the claims and is currently evaluating legal remedies to challenge the award. The hospitality firm, valued at $9 billion, said that even with the legal battle, Zo 'continues to misrepresent and latch on to OYO'.

OYO said that the arbitration hasn't given any direction for issuance of shares as the definitive agreement was neither agreed upon nor consummated and therefore closing conditions were far from being achieved.

"The Tribunal has ruled and categorically acknowledged that the definitive agreements, which are extremely important documents for any M&A transaction, were neither finalised nor agreed upon," read OYO's statement.

Here's a look at the timeline of events

2015: OYO's lead investor SoftBank in its annual report claims that the Ritesh Agarwal-led startup had acquired its rival Zo Rooms.

September, 2016: Merger talks between the two companies fall through.

2017: OYO confirms that it has ended all discussions in the matter and says, "we tried to identify potential value in their business but could not reach an outcome".

2018: Zo Rooms takes OYO to court claiming 'data theft' while doing the due diligence during the acquisition talks.

February, 2018: Gurugram court hands the ruling in favor of OYO. Zo Rooms says it doesn't have the financial bandwidth to 'incur prolonged legal costs'. However, soon after Zo approached the Supreme Court.

October, 2018: Supreme Court appoints a three-judge bench to evaluate the matter.

January, 2020: Zo Rooms once again files a plea over OYO's restructuring of its board, saying that the restructuring will hamper Zo's claims of 7% stake in OYO.

March, 2021: The tribunal said that Zo Rooms parent Zostel Hospitality was entitled to claim relief and costs in the case, however acknowledged that definitive agreements weren't executed.

It's not just Zostel, OYO has 20 other lawsuits to fight

- OYO has 21 cases registered against the company, subsidiaries, directors, and promoters.
- The company has spent nearly ₹1,166 crore as legal and professional fees in the last three financial years.
- It also estimates that any adverse outcome in legal proceedings involving Zostel, may adversely impact their business.

The extensive list of lawsuits against hotel and hospitality giant OYO is no secret. As the company has grown, so have the cases being filed against it. And the company does not expect this number to go down any sooner.

OYO — in its draft red herring prospectus (DRHP) for the $1.2 billion initial public offering (IPO) — had noted that the number of legal disputes and proceedings against the company may continue to increase as the company scales further.

It is important to note that OYO has 21 cases registered against it, its subsidiaries, its directors, and its promoters.

the This includes the petition filed by Federation of Hotels and Restaurants the Association of India (FHRAI) in front of Competition Commission of India (CCI) against MakeMyTrip, Goibibo and OYO for dominating the online travel agents (OTA) market. Treebo Hotels has raised similar allegations against the company.

As per the DRHP, the company has spent nearly ₹1,166 crore as legal and professional fees in the last three financial years.

"The number and significance of these claims, disputes, and proceedings have increased as our Company has grown larger, the number of bookings on our platform has increased, our brand awareness has increased and the scope and complexity of our business have expanded, and we expect that the number and significance of such claims, disputes and proceedings will continue to increase," OYO's DRHP revealed.

The filing also noted that there are no outstanding litigation proceedings involving any OYO group companies that "have a material impact on our company".

9th ALLEGATION

Oyo Hotel Room Death Case: Man Strangled Woman & Then Died By Suicide In Delhi

Days after a couple was found dead in Oyo hotel room in east Delhi's Maujpur area, the autopsy report has revealed that the woman was strangled to death while the man committed suicide after killing her, an officer said on Thursday. The bodies of Sohrab, 28, a resident of Uttar Pradesh's Meerut, and Ayesha, 27, a resident of Loni were found in the Oyo hotel room on October 27.

The cause of death of the woman was ligature strangulation

"During the post-mortem examination, doctors found that the cause of death of the woman (Ayesha) was ligature strangulation. The cause of death of the man (Sohrab) was suicidal hanging," said the Deputy Commissioner of Police (northeast) Joy Tirkey.

A call was received regarding two bodies in King's Stay Oyo Hotel

According to police, on October 27, at 8.05 p.m, a call was received regarding two bodies in King's Stay Oyo Hotel following which a police team rushed to the spot. "It was found that Sohrab and Ayesha had checked in at the Oyo Hotel at 1.02 p.m. and had booked the room for four hours," said the DCP. When they did not come out, the hotel staff knocked on the door at about 7:45 p.m.

Sohrab was found hanging from the ceiling fan

"There was no response so they called the Beat Constable. The room was opened in the presence of the police and Sohrab was found hanging from the ceiling fan with a nylon rope. Ayesha was found lying dead on the bed. There were some ligature marks on her neck.

Suicide note was found lying on the bed

"A half-page hand written (in Hindi) suicide note was found lying on the bed next to Ayesha, claiming that both were in love and had decided to end their lives together," the DCP said. "A case of murder has been registered after a post-mortem report. Further investigation is in progress," said the DCP.

Controversy

Fine in the United States

Agarwal signed agreements through his company OYO with hotel owners in the US in which the buildings of the owners will be rebranded under the OYO name in exchange for compensation and guarantee income but left out the information that OYO is not authorized to operate franchise business in the state of California for which in March 2019, OYO was fined $200,000 by California regulators. The company also received a cease and desist order from Washington, after regulators found OYO made offers to many hotel owners and managers, without proper registration.

WHAT YOU HAVE LEARNT NOW, MAKE SOME NOTES SO THAT YOU CANNOT FORGET

CHAPTER 8
SOME UNKNOWN STORIES AND MINDBLOWING DATA

"THE THING WITH NEW EXPERIENCES IS THAT IT TURNS OUT TO BE EITHER GOOD OR BAD. DO YOU HAVE A GOOD ONE? THAT'S GREAT! HAD A BAD ONE? YOU WILL END UP LEARNING FROM IT AND AT THE END IMPROVE YOURSELF AS A PERSON"

ADITYA GHOSH ON OYO

When Aditya Ghosh left IndiGo in April 2018, he could have joined any big company with a legacy. After careful consideration, he chose OYO Hotels & Homes, which its 25-year-old founder Ritesh Agarwal has taken from being a start-up to a company valued at $5 billion and present in 10 countries.

Everybody wanted to know the logic behind Ghosh's decision to join OYO as its CEO (India and South Asia). To find out, we met the 42-year-old at Delhi's India Habitat Centre moments after the company announced a commitment of Rs 1,400 crore ($200m) for the India and South Asia business as part of expansion plans and to improve customer experience.

On a lawyer becoming CEO

First I studied science and math in school. Then history and then law. As a lawyer, you are trained in a way to declutter and come back to what is important for that particular case on that particular day. You are trained to look for a needle in the haystack. Having said that, my biggest learnings have been with the leaders I have worked with. And more importantly, the line folks I got to work and interact with. I am ever curious, constantly asking questions. I always want to learn something new. I am ever grateful for the people around me, be it at the airline or today. The amount of patience people show answering my questions, I have always benefitted from.

ADVERTISEMENT

On meeting Ritesh Agarwal

I met him in early-August for the first time. We bumped into each other at award functions and things like that but we didn't know each other nor did we have each other's numbers. He often says that I was constantly talking myself out of the job. Frankly, I was not meeting him for a job. We met to exchange ideas and discuss some challenges. I just couldn't see why he would need someone else to come and partner with him. He has got a great leadership team, nothing is broken in the business, he is growing at a phenomenal scale, attracting talent left, right and center. And more than anything else, he was (then) just 24 years old. So he was not tired!

We could connect at a level where there was no pressure. In the first two days we spent 13 hours with each other and then we had a series of conversations. What became obvious was the chemistry between the two. What is important is that we are not identical people — we have different interests in food, music and films. But dare I say that we are also very complementary.

The ah-ha moment came when I realized two things — on one hand it is a similar business (customer, market segments, price points) but it also pushed me completely out of my comfort zone because it has nothing to do with the airline business. And then, for the first time, we have this once-in-a-lifetime opportunity to create a brand out of India that's truly global. You can go buy a KitKat in Asansol, Durgapur, Roorkee and Chikmagalur but can you go to the Midwest in the US or the interiors of Europe and find an Indian brand in a street corner? After having the phenomenal opportunity in my previous job, where I was able to be a part of a story where you can create from scratch a world-recognised brand from India, this opportunity fell into my lap... of creating a global brand this time, which hopefully will have consistency in terms of quality, reach and depth.

On holidaying between jobs

I was camping in the interiors of Kashmir... no glamping. It was serious camping, complete with cooking on wood fire. My exposure to OYO was when one day, Ritesh, at 11.30 at night, said let's go and see a few properties. We made bookings on the OYO app and showed up at some hotels in Delhi and Gurgaon. Finally, on one of those nights, at around 1.30am I told him let's go and see the office. We landed up at the OYO office; nobody was there and the guards didn't recognize us. Further, he didn't have his identity card. So we walked down to the basement and then to the 12th floor.

There is a terrace there and we spent two hours walking up and down while talking.

On the unlearning curve,

I come from the background of one brand and one product and one type of service. And everything gets built around that. It took some time to understand the logic and now I am a big champion of it... about why we should have a multi-brand strategy. For a CEO of a low-cost carrier, who constantly talked of one product, to now come in and say, no, seven brands may work or even 20 brands may work... is a different experience. The way the customer behaves here is very different because they are divided by price point, they are divided geographically, they are divided by demographic.... So you already have a matrix.

Then you think that the same customer one day has a certain need when he is with his kids, another day he has different needs when he is with college friends. When you put all these probabilities into a grid, there are a large bunch of possibilities. What do legacy hospitality businesses do? They say, we will have this number of blocks or pigeonholes and you either fit in or don't. We are doing the exact opposite. We will say if there are 16 possibilities, we will address all 16; we will take on that additional complexity; we will create different brands and price points; we will take the brand to where you are. This was a major learning and to some extent an unlearning.

On Bangla and being a Bengali

My favorite food in the world is posto. I work out intensely — I do weight training — at Rabindra Sangeet! That may sound really strange. I take a lot of pride in my heritage. My wife is a Punjabi, my sister-in-law is a Tamilian. We speak Bangla at home. Here is an interesting story. I grew up in Delhi and so I studied English and Hindi. As a kid, whenever there were arguments, I argued in English because I was thinking in English. My mother told me, if you have to argue, argue in Bangla. At home, I speak Bangla. I was born in Calcutta but I was brought up in Delhi. But my summer vacations were spent in Calcutta. Everybody in the family, other than my parents, still lives in Calcutta.

IT'S SHOWTIME AS STAKES GET HIGHER FOR OYO

In November 2018, Oyo (Oravel Stays Pvt. Ltd) announced the appointment of **Aditya Ghosh** as chief executive officer (CEO) of its South Asia business. Ghosh's appointment was a coup for Oyo, as impressive as the $5 billion valuation it had secured in a large funding round three months ago.

Ghosh was one of the most sought-after corporate leaders, having won universal acclaim for his performance as CEO of India's largest airline IndiGo. Ghosh's "business acumen, his problem-solving capabilities, and his customer-centric approach to innovation that helped him build an influential brand that is loved by all, makes him an excellent choice", Oyo founder and CEO Ritesh Agarwal said last November.

Barely a year later, Ghosh resigned from his position, to be replaced by Rohit Kapoor, another senior Oyo executive. Earlier this week, **Oyo** said that Ghosh will become a director on its board and termed the move an "elevation" for him.

Agarwal's statement explaining the move echoed his words from last year. "Aditya's strong business acumen, problem-solving capabilities, passion for building an organization with strong corporate governance, and a high-performing work culture that thrives on principles of diversity and inclusion, makes him the perfect choice for this larger and more strategic role, at a global level," Agarwal said on 2 December.

But according to two people familiar with the matter, Ghosh's exit as CEO and his move to the board wasn't what the company had in mind when he was appointed last year. Ghosh's move to a non-operational role was an admission that the decision to hire him hadn't worked out for both parties, said the people cited above.

"At Oyo, the power lies with Ritesh and a small group of senior leaders who have been at the company for many years. Aditya was on cordial terms with Ritesh but his management style was different, and he was never part of this circle. He was struggling to have the kind of authority and influence that he had enjoyed at IndiGo," said one of the two people cited above.

Oyo disputes this account. Ghosh achieved key targets such as improving service, safety and security at Oyo properties, and others ahead of time, said the company. It added that Ghosh will now play a bigger, global role and his move will strengthen its board of directors.

"India has doubled in size in the last one year, and our margins have improved considerably for the India and South Asia business. To meet the changing business requirements, multiple leaders have been expected to 'step-up' and play a larger role. Many leaders, therefore, have been promoted in the organisation, and Aditya's elevation is no exception," an Oyo spokesperson said in an email.

The expansion spree

Ghosh's exit comes as Oyo is in the midst of a historic expansion spree. Over the past two years, it has launched in dozens of countries and spent hundreds of millions of dollars buying hotel firms. Since September 2017, the pioneering startup has raised $2.5 billion and seen its valuation soar to $10 billion.

In recent memory, no other Indian consumer company, much less an internet startup, has ventured with such gusto into difficult international markets like China, the UK and US all at the same time.

Within 18 months of entering China, Oyo established itself as the second-largest hotel chain in that country with about 9,000 properties on its platform. In India, it is by far the largest hotel chain with about 18,000 properties. In May, Oyo bought Amsterdam-based @Leisure Group for more than $400 million. It spent $135 million to buy the Hooters Casino Hotel in Las Vegas in August. Oyo has also been expanding its Townhouse brand, and entering new businesses like food and office sharing.

But, suddenly, just as the company closed a landmark funding deal that saw Agarwal triple his stake to 30%, Oyo is facing a moment of reckoning.

After a long funding boom, US startups such as WeWork Companies Inc., Uber Technologies Inc., and Lyft Inc., which had binged on capital, have received a reality check from public markets. Japanese technology and investment firm SoftBank Group Corp., which has been at the forefront of the startup funding boom, is facing hurdles in raising its second $100 billion fund. The impact of these developments is now spilling over to Indian startups that have spent billions of dollars to expand, but are nowhere near profitability.

Oyo is near the top of the list of companies whose unprofitable business models are being scrutinized by investors and analysts. Questions are being raised about its headlong expansion in China and whether the company has moved too soon without a sufficient understanding of the local market. In India, too, there are concerns about its ability to retain hotel partners as it increases commission rates to improve margins.

Oyo versus WeWork

The most topical concern about Oyo, however, is its apparent likeness with WeWork, the office sharing startup that has seen a plunge in valuation and required a $9.5 billion bailout by SoftBank in October to stay afloat.

Critics say that Oyo and WeWork have many similarities: both are in execution-heavy real estate businesses, a fact that isn't reflected in their valuations, which are in keeping with those of internet firms; both have expanded recklessly without proving their business models can become profitable; and both have used large quantities of capital to paper over weaknesses in their models.

These viewpoints are reflected, to an extent, in Oyo's numbers. According to a valuation report filed with the Registrar of Companies last month, Oyo's revenues rose to ₹6,457 crore in FY19 from ₹1,413 crore in the previous year. But total expenditure also jumped to ₹9,027.53 crore in FY19 from ₹1,835.38 crore a year ago. These are unaudited financials, but they give an indication of the cost of Oyo's expansion.

Critics also point out that WeWork's disastrous expansion was possible only because of the close relationship between SoftBank founder Masayoshi Son and Adam Neumann, co-founder and CEO of WeWork. Similarly, the Japanese billionaire has been known to say that he sees Agarwal as a "son". SoftBank owns 48% in Oravel Stays, the company which runs Oyo. Agarwal's $2 billion share transaction in Oyo was funded by loans backed by Son personally, according to earlier reports in *Mint* and other publications.

At a closer look, however, Oyo's business model differs from WeWork's in important aspects. Oyo doesn't have billions of dollars due in lease payments to office landlords that nearly crippled WeWork earlier this year.

The major upfront payments that Oyo makes to its hotel partners are "minimum business guarantees" that it uses to lure new hotels. These costs reduce over time as occupancy rates increase. Oyo requires far less capital to grow than WeWork did.

Their raisons d'être are fundamentally different, too. WeWork is creating a new kind of office environment that is significantly different from the way corporates have been used to working. Oyo, on the other hand, is more of a classic efficiency-increasing internet platform that makes a sector—hotel bookings and stays—more efficient and predictable by using technology.

Agarwal, too, has been stressing privately that the personal excesses of Neumann and the corporate governances issues found at WeWork are absent at Oyo. The 26-year-old also makes it a point to seek mentoring and advice from experienced corporate leaders such as former managing director of Bharti Airtel Ltd Manoj Kohli, who is now the executive chairman of SB Energy Corp., SoftBank's renewable energy initiative.

Issues of dominance

Actually, the difficulties facing Oyo in daily operations are similar to those that dog all internet marketplaces: balancing the interests of suppliers and consumers.

Over the past six months, as Oyo has become increasingly dominant in the budget hotel space, the firm has been hiking commission rates. Some hotels that *Mint* spoke to said that Oyo charges commission rates (including fees and charges) of more than 40%. A few hundred hotels have left the platform recently.

Oyo maintains that only a small fraction of its overall supplier base have irresolvable differences with the company and most of the hotels on its platform continue to have a working relationship with the firm.

Still, problems with suppliers are bound to increase. As capital becomes scarcer and pricier in the post-WeWork era, Oyo will have to constantly find ways to cut losses. A senior Oyo executive, speaking on condition of anonymity, said that the company will avoid raising prices and instead continue to increase "operating efficiencies".

But an investor in the hotels space pointed out that it will be tough for Oyo to sustain its present room rates, which in many properties are less than half of the listed price.

"The only way (they can sustain the current prices) is by getting more money from hotels. But if you overdo that, then working with Oyo becomes an unattractive proposition for hotel owners," said the investor.

Oyo's troubles with some of its suppliers, and investor concerns about the unprofitable unicorns in general, have come as a boon for two of its smaller Indian rivals, Treebo Hotels and FabHotels. Late last year, the two firms were battling for survival—and even considered merging but eventually decided against it.

But over the past three-four months, both Treebo and FabHotels have seen a sharp increase in sales growth, said a person familiar with the matter. Treebo executives have a term for hotels that it lost to Oyo last year only for them to return: "*ghar wapsi*". Including these hotels, Treebo has poached a few hundred properties in the past six months from Oyo, said the person cited above, on condition of anonymity.

Despite the recent improvement in sales, however, Treebo and FabHotels remain far smaller in size. The two firms together have less than 2,000 properties, compared with 18,000 for Oyo India. Fundraising for Treebo and FabHotels will continue to be difficult because of Oyo's dominance.

But Oyo doesn't look invincible any more. In late October, the Competition Commission of India said it will investigate whether Oyo and MakeMyTrip violated competition rules following a complaint from the Federation of Hotel and Restaurant Associations of India.

China holds key

A large part of Oyo's $10 billion valuation has to do with its international expansion, especially in the China market. China is a far bigger market than India and demand for budget hotels is growing rapidly.

Accordingly, Oyo has expanded at a dizzying rate. It already has 9,000 properties in Asia's largest economy.

But two people familiar with the matter said that Oyo's occupancy rates in China were less than 40%, compared with its average occupancy rates in India that hover between 60% and 70%. The company also encountered fraudulent behaviour by some of its China employees and hotel partners as it lacked controls and processes in the first year of operations.

The Oyo spokesperson confirmed that its China properties had low occupancy rates earlier, but said that they have picked up after the company introduced a new model called Oyo 2.0 in May 2019 for its China hotel suppliers. Under this model, Oyo provides technology tools, capital for improving properties and other support to its suppliers. Since its introduction, Oyo's average occupancy rates have jumped to 75%, said the spokesperson. Oyo has also fired some employees and instituted stronger internal controls over the past few months.

While Oyo has established itself as one of the top two hotel chains in China in terms of size, it has seen tepid interest among local Chinese investors. Two Chinese firms, Didi Chuxing Technology Co. and Huazhu Group, have invested in Oyo, but have together put up less than $150 million of the $2.5 billion raised by the company in the last two funding rounds.

Huazhu Group is also Oyo's chief rival in China. Its H Hotels brand has been competing in the budget hotel space with Oyo. Huazhu, which is listed on Nasdaq, is a licensee of hotel brands across price segments.

Oyo has bulldozed its way to the top of the Chinese market by splurging capital and is far bigger than H Hotels, but Huazhu's overall numbers give an indication of the slower, profit-focused approach that publicly-listed firms need to adopt to please markets.

In 2018, Huazhu reported revenues of $1.46 billion, an increase of 22% over 2017. Its net profit in 2018 was $106 million.

In the first three quarters of 2019, the Chinese hospitality firm's revenues have risen just 10% over a year ago, according to its published results. Huazhu's market capitalization is around $10 billion—the same as Oyo's.

When asked whether Oyo will continue to prioritize growth over margins, the Oyo spokesperson said that the company "has heard the market. We have always been on the path of profitability and are committed to financial prudence with a focus on sustainable growth".

MYSTERY OF OYO ROOMS

First, it laid off about 20 percent of its 12,000-strong staff in India by the end-2019, and cut down 5 percent of the 12,000-strong workforce in China as part of a restructuring. In India, it pulled out operations from 200 of the 600 cities. Just as the world was coming to grips with the sudden scale-down at the fast-growing Oyo Hotels & Homes, more retrenchments were announced at the US operations.

Meanwhile, the anger and dissatisfaction among hotel partners continues to swell. Reports suggest that nearly 500 hotel partners, of about 20,000, have snapped ties with the company since April 2019, alleging hidden charges and lack of transparency (though Oyo claims its partner churn is less than 1 per cent). On top of that, earlier this year, the Income

Tax Department arrived at its Gurgaon headquarters to inspect the books of accounts, which the company called a "regular TDS audit".

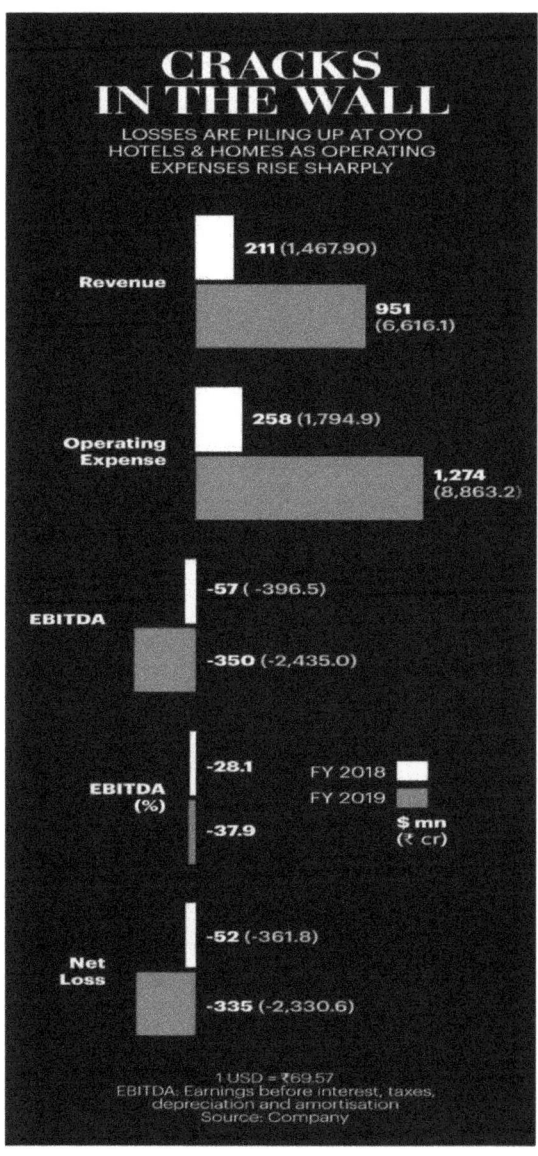

Since the beginning of 2019, a raft of bad news emerging from Oyo has raised a question mark over the company's astounding growth story. Last year, a major controversy erupted around Founder Ritesh Agarwal's decision to buy back shares at a whopping $10 billion-valuation from the money lent by three Japanese financial institutions that are reportedly close to its lead investor SoftBank. The share buyback doubled Oyo's valuation - and made investor SoftBank less miserable after the WeWork debacle - despite no major improvement in the underlying business.

Oyo's business model of capturing market share and building scale is hinged on enormous cash-burn - primarily funded by marquee investors such as SoftBank, Sequoia Capital, Lightspeed Venture Partners, and most recently, Airbnb. The hotel chain has been reporting net losses for several years in a row (see table Cracks in the Wall). Losses increased from $52 million in FY18 to $335 million in FY19, according to the company.

With the firm still to declare a deadline to profits, cost cuts became inevitable. The dramatic cut in staff strength in India and abroad point to a desperate effort to slash costs after an unsuccessful attempt at building a roadmap to profitability.

Has the unique hotel platform begun to falter after an unbridled run?

After all, these events undermine the Oyo story its founder Agarwal had envisaged. Agarwal told Business Today in a meeting last year that Oyo was on its way to becoming the largest hotel chain in the world by 2023 (by room inventory) led by three pillars: customers, employees, and the leadership team. But in a recent meeting with BT, Oyo's newly-appointed CEO (for India and South Asia), Rohit

Kapoor, hinted that the ambition may be out of reach now: "Everybody has a right to change their plans". So, has Oyo given up on its grand plans?

Caught Speeding

There are indications that Oyo may be faltering. While there was always a question mark over its break-neck speed of adding hotels to the platform at the expense of service quality, the expansion over the past three years has hit a speed breaker, especially in India and China, its largest markets. Today, Oyo operates in over 800 cities in 80 countries - a huge ramp-up for a start-up that was set up only in 2013. Not just that, it has pivoted its model several times besides rapidly diversifying into areas such as co-living, co-working, vacation homes, tour packaging, cloud kitchen, weddings and cafes.

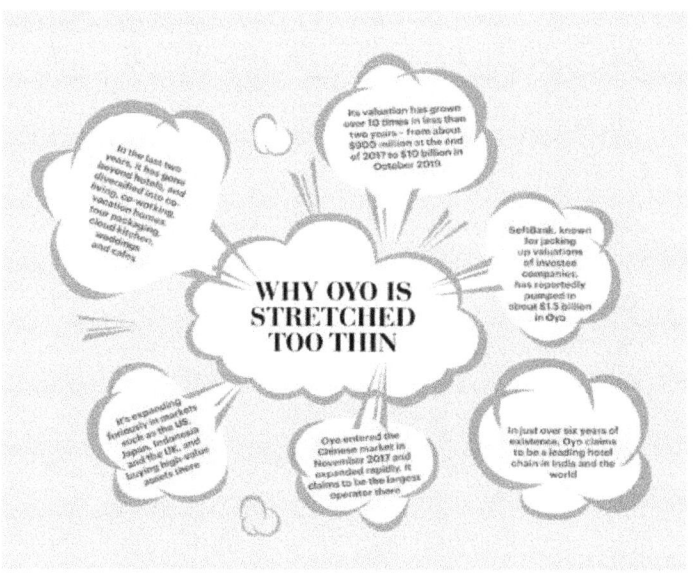

"They are in a space that nobody understands because never in the history of our industry has somebody grown so quickly. Theirs is a story that will unfold with time. But what one sees with interest is their audacity to be able to do this," says Manav Thadani, Co-founder of hotel consultancy Hotelivate.

As part of the company's recent restructuring, which invited a lot of undue attention, some of the businesses have been brought under a single leadership structure. For instance, its frontier businesses Oyo Townhouse, Collection O, Oyo Life and Oyo Home were separate verticals. These were combined in December 2019, and brought under the leadership of Ankit Gupta, a former senior partner at McKinsey, who joined Oyo in the same month. "I don't think we are exiting any business right now," says Kapoor, rubbishing reports of the company's likely exit from the weddings business, and reported merger of co-living business (Oyo Life) with the flagship hotels (Oyo Rooms) vertical.

Overpromise, Underdeliver

During the heydays of the tech giant Infosys under Co-founder N.R. Narayana Murthy was a favorite of the stock markets for a simple reason. Like other tech companies, Infosys would give guidance to investors, and in almost every quarter, the published results were better than the outlook given in the previous quarter. Infosys was playing with the psyche of the investors, and in turn, they rewarded it disproportionately.

"The important change is not that we set a deadline... But to make sure that through the restructuring exercise, we go back to the basics and say which parts of the business will make money structurally "

- Rohit Kapoor
(CEO India and South Asia Oyo)

The story playing out at the aggregator-turned-hotel-chain Oyo is quite the opposite. Over the past four-odd years, it has become the poster boy of the Indian start-up scene, and has drawn a lot of attention. In October, its valuation touched $10 billion that made it the second-most valuable start-up in the country after Vijay Shekhar Sharma-controlled Paytm (valued at around $16 billion). In just over two years, Oyo's valuation has grown more than 10 times, and since September 2018, it has doubled.

Though Japanese investment firm SoftBank first invested around $100 million in Oyo in 2015, the big break came in September 2018 when it poured another $1 billion along with other investors. This put Oyo on the global stage - not just within the start-up and PE/VC community but also in actual presence.

Since then, Oyo has expanded furiously beyond India into markets like China, the US, Japan, Indonesia and the UK. In China, for instance, where it entered in November 2017, it became the largest single hotel brand last June. Between January and June 2019, its room count in China more than doubled to over 500,000. In the US, it crossed the 100-hotel milestone in September across 60 cities. "The US is fastest growing for Oyo. Every night I go to sleep, there's one Oyo hotel that opens in the US," Agarwal told an audience at the THINC Indonesia 2019 conference last September.

Oyo now boasts of being the world's leading chain of hotels and homes. Its combined portfolio, in late January, comprised more than 43,000 hotels with over 1 million rooms. In December, the number of hotels stood at 44,000, and a month before that, it was 35,000. Surprisingly, the number of rooms has stayed the same in all these months.

As per a valuation report filed with India's Ministry of Corporate Affairs (MCA) last year, Oyo reported that it would turn profitable by 2022 - a projection that has been rejected by nearly every industry analyst. "I think no such target has been set. Like any other business, we create an annual operating plan... The important change is not that we set a deadline - because that's artificial - but to make sure that through the restructuring exercise of the last two months, we have gone back to the basics and said which parts of the business will make money structurally. Now it's a question of executing and getting the team along and executing to that outcome," says CEO Kapoor, adding that Oyo is already profitable in some businesses. For instance, says Kapoor, at business EBITDA (earnings before interest, tax, depreciation and amortization) level, co-working and homes businesses are profitable. "In some other parts, it may happen in three to nine months. We are willing to make that investment," he adds.

A major focus area for the company needs to be customer experience. A disgruntled customer even started a website (oyo-ruined-my-anniversary.com) to share his bad experience with Oyo. A common strain in complaints is poor quality of rooms and services, and that the rooms don't match what appears on the app.

"What has gone wrong for them is that they still haven't got their hands on quality control, which is why a large number of guests are complaining of service issues at their hotels," says Hotelivate's Thadani.

To get things in order, Oyo will need to make more changes. "Oyo's business strategy requires a shift from a singular focus on growth and scale to operational efficiencies, customer experience, workforce training and much improved asset management leading to improved yields. A company that claims to be the second-largest hotel player globally by number of rooms cannot use that as its calling card without stopping its cash burn and demonstrating its ability to be profitable," says Mandeep Lamba, President, HVS Anarock, the South Asia arm of global hospitality consulting firm HVS.

OYO FACTBOX

Founded in
2013

Global headcount:
25,000

Global asset owner partners:
43,000

Number of hotel rooms globally:
1 million+

Number of rooms in India:
300,000 across 17,000 hotels

Number of Oyo rooms booked per second (in 2019):
5

Global Oyo app user base (2019):
77.5 million

A leading hospitality consultant, who did not wish to be named, said their numbers are opaque about a lot of things and the company is likely to be a long way from earning a profit. On being asked about profitability in Indonesia in September, Agarwal had said, "It's hard for me to give guidance about the potential timeframe. At the building level, we are making margins worldwide. We are investing heavily on the corporate side... On an year-on-year basis, our net losses have reduced by 50 per cent." The numbers, however, tell a different tale.

Agarwal likes to compare Oyo with Marriott International, Hilton Hotels and IHG, but the truth is that it's nowhere close to these global chains. Marriott's room inventory is over 1.3 million (slightly higher than Oyo), but the company registered revenues of $20.76 billion and profits of $2.2 billion in 2018. In comparison, Oyo reported revenues of just $951 million in FY19 and losses of $335 million, as per the latest numbers declared by the company.

One may argue that Oyo is a start-up, and a comparison with legacy operators like Marriott is unfair. But since Oyo has ambitions to lead the global hospitality market at some point in future, all parameters, including revenues and profits, are under the scanner. "We are opening 14 times more keys worldwide in comparison to Marriott, Hilton and IHG combined. It is not a fair comparison because IHG is primarily in economy and mid-scale, and Hilton is primarily mid-scale; we are primarily economy. It's not the most like-to-like comparison but that's the closest comparison that we could find," Agarwal said.

According to a hotel association member, Oyo could have perhaps avoided many of its troubles by just operating at a low key, however that route would have gone against its valuation game.

Bed of Thorns

Back in 2013, Oyo actually started off as a full-service hotel operator. But it was competing with Zo Rooms, Treebo and Fab Hotels that were aggregators. All these players were fighting for the same kind of supply. Thanks to the aggregation model, where operators take part in inventory in a hotel, Oyo's competitors were signing up more hotels. This led to Oyo pivoting into aggregation in 2015. The scalability in aggregation was faster as mom-and-pop hotels were guaranteed income on their leased rooms. In any case, a part of their inventory always remained unsold. Many online travel agents like MakeMyTrip, Goibibo and others had also followed a similar model, but pulled out later.

Oyo's plan was to ensure minimum service standards, put its branding, and sell it on the app at rates between Rs 1,500 and Rs 3,000, which is affordable to a bulk of travelers. The branded hotel market in India was an inverted pyramid for long where luxury and upscale hotels had the largest share. But things have changed over the past 10 years with a significant mid-scale and budget inventory coming into the market.

Broadly, hotels in India fall in three categories: branded legal hotels, standalone unbranded but legal hotels, and guest houses which are not always legal. The unbranded legal hotels are estimated to be below one million rooms while the guest houses are about two million. Oyo is focusing on these two categories. "Who needs Oyo? The person who cannot sell because his location is wrong or product is lousy or there's too much competition or he is not distributing well. Oyo can probably help in distribution," says a mid-scale hotel promoter.

Back to another pivot. By 2016, Oyo had become a dominant player - backed by funding from marquee investors like Sequoia Capital and Lightspeed Ventures - and had nearly killed all its competitors. It pivoted again; this time to becoming a hotel operator.

Over the past three years, Oyo has gone one by one to 10,000-plus hotels, and moved them from the aggregation structure to a manchised model (franchise with a general manager), taking full inventory under its control. While the managers are deputed by Oyo and their allegiance lies with the company, the salary comes from the property owners. Oyo has moved as much as 85-90 per cent of its total inventory to this model to build scale.

Interestingly, this 85-90 per cent inventory (called Oyo Rooms in India) put together does not generate even 25-30 percent of the company's total revenue, experts say. The other 10-15 per cent inventory is in the new projects that the company has started over the past three years. This includes Oyo Townhouse, SilverKey, Capital O, Edition O, Palette

Resorts and Oyo Flagship. All the newer brands are either management contracts or leases - the traditional models followed by the branded hotels segment.

Large chains like Hyatt Hotels, Marriott International, Accor and others are operating most of their properties under management contracts. In a management deal, the hotel owner keeps the profit and pays a fee to the hotel brand. In a lease, the brand pays rent to the owner, and keeps the profit. Less aggressive hotel owners typically choose the lease model.

"They still haven't got their hands on quality control which is why guests are complaining of service issues "

**- Manav Thadani
(Co-founder, Hotelivate)**

"Most of their million-plus rooms are still under the franchisee model. They have put all their new brands under one of these two models (leased or managed). About 65-70 per cent of their revenues are believed to come from the new brands. These are also the models they will grow domestically," says a hotel consultant, not wishing to be named.

But why pursue the manchise model when it is generating poor revenues? That's because the model gives them scale, marketing muscle, visibility, and boasting rights to be the world's leading hotel company. Experts say the company might see this manchising turning into leasing or managing at some point. "The scale is with them. If they are able to prove to owners across thousands of hotels that the new models are profitable, they will be able to convert the bulk of the inventory," says a hotel consultant quoted above.

But the problem with the manchisee model is more than just low revenues and profits. In order to keep these hotels under its fold, Oyo has to constantly burn money in deep discounting, which is where it's getting a bad name. Take an example. An average guest who always stayed at a particular hotel used to pay Rs 1,800 a night to it. The property owner tied up with Oyo, which is now selling the same room at Rs 999 on its app. The same guest now books through Oyo. The owner complains to Oyo for selling rooms at such huge discounts. Oyo, in return, says that it's reimbursing the difference from its pocket, and there's no reason for owners to grumble. The problem is that Oyo is perhaps eroding the market: the customer is getting used to the Rs 999 price. What happens when the cash-burn stops?

"Hotel owners believe that they are at the mercy of Oyo. Online travel agents and e-commerce companies have been deep discounting. People are saying that this is not in the spirit of fair market conditions. Oyo is getting rapped for that," says a senior executive at a large OTA.

Oyo, however, claims that the actual room prices - prices that customers are willing to pay - tend to be lower than the owners' self-assessed rates. The start-up looks at RevPAR (revenue per available room) - an industry metric which is a combination of rates and occupancy, rather than just tariffs - to drive growth for its partners. Oyo says that once it takes over a hotel, occupancy shoots up substantially. So, even if room tariffs are lower than before, overall revenues of that property grow.

Up in Arms

Not just deep discounting, a half-dozen hotel owners that BT spoke with said that employees at the local level are using unfair means to increase hotel sign-ups. Oyo's staff, they say, are being given impractically high targets, which is forcing local teams to get contracts signed without disclosing full terms to the owners. Small hotel owners trust the Oyo name, and sign contracts without reading or understanding the fine print.

Last September, Delhi-based hotel operator Vijay Tiwari became the leader of 'victimized' owners in Delhi's hospitality hub Paharganj. After being allegedly cheated by Oyo, Tiwari made a video asking other hoteliers to boycott Oyo. The video went viral, and nearly 90 hotel owners in the vicinity joined the protests. Oyo slapped cases against some owners, but later asked for more time from the court to pursue these cases.

"Oyo's business strategy requires a shift from a singular focus on growth and scale to operational efficiencies," Mandeep Lamba

(President, HVS Anarock)

Tiwari had signed the contract for three properties with Oyo last February. "Initially, I was told that Oyo would sell 5-10 rooms out of each property, and they had also set the floor price. We signed the deal at 12.5 percent commission with no hidden charges," he says. Tiwari's contract with Oyo, which BT reviewed, was a franchisee agreement for his entire inventory, and not for partial inventory that he says the Oyo executive had promised. Tiwari also claims that Oyo used a different name on its app to sell these hotels so that he could sell his inventory on other platforms as well. "Oyo started penalizing me for not honoring the contract. It's only after we went to court that we realized that they had all the rights on our properties," he says. "They were penalizing me (for selling part inventory on my own) more than the business it was generating for me. After four months, they told me that the penalty cannot be reversed as their policy has changed. I emailed but they stopped replying. They have not refunded the amount yet," he says.

The tribe of distressed hotel partners is growing, making it another big problem that Oyo has to deal with. In September, for instance, an FIR was reportedly filed against Agarwal by Bengaluru hotelier Natarajan V.R.S. accusing the company of unfair business practices. Less than two months after that, another Bengaluru hotelier, Betz Fernandez, reportedly filed a case of cheating against Agarwal and six others alleging non-payment of rent for rooms for five months. There are over a dozen WhatsApp groups of Oyo 'victims' (this writer is member of two groups) where hoteliers across the country share latest developments on Oyo, and the status of their varied complaints against the chain. One analyst says that since many of these are small businesses, they don't have pockets deep enough to wait for six months for payments.

Oyo's Kapoor admits that issues at the local level is an area where the company has to improve. "There are two factors to it. Do my [employees at the] last-mile understand the product they are selling? The second is simplification at every level. The core [issue] is around both sides understanding what it takes to run the partnership because there are obligations on both sides," he says.

Credibility at Stake

The company's accountability in the industry is also taking a beating as many hoteliers say that Oyo artificially pumps up its number of rooms. They say the number of available rooms is actually much less because Oyo doesn't unlist properties even after the contract with them has ended. A case in point is Delhi's Capital O 22145 Hotel BB Palace, which snapped ties with Oyo last October, but was still listed on the app - although the booking status stated it was 'sold off' - at the time of writing the story.

Another hotelier, requesting anonymity, accused the company of having a lot of fake listings. "Oyo doesn't ask for any legal documents or hotel license. They just ask for bank details, GST number and PAN card. Several of their properties have duplicate listings on other platforms. I am still getting reconciliation statements for bookings months after ending the contract with them," he says.

But that was not the case a while ago; earlier many property owners were eager to sign up. Oyo convinced small-time hotel owners to follow its model. The playbook was set: Oyo would take over unproductive assets, renovate them with good design, operate them well, and boost the occupancies. Agarwal told BT in 2019 that the assets that joined Oyo's network saw occupancy go up from 25 per cent to 75 percent in a maximum of three months. In markets like India, the lead time is just a month. And despite the rise in occupancy, the cost didn't rise much - 10 per cent maybe - which resulted in a 15-16 times jump in profits for hoteliers.

This is also the formula that Oyo has followed in other countries. "Once they make a strategic decision to enter a country, they are able to scale up fast. They are process driven. Credit goes to them for having created tech-based platforms that enable everything from signing up a hotel in 48 hours to opening it in 14 days to actually doing Greenfield development in less than a year. They have software for revenue management, quality assurance, yield management, and distribution. All of this is developed by a team of about 1,600 data scientists, who are coders with a business mind," says Hotelivate's Thadani.

Then why are hotel partners leaving Oyo now? The start-up says that it's largely because owners are not able to deliver quality experience to guests. "It is often about the customer service standards that we expect from partners. A large part of our partner base does a fantastic job of serving the customer. But a small part is not able to match up to the requirement. When that happens, we have to take them off the network till they make the correction and come back," Kapoor says, adding that he is personally meeting 2-3 unhappy partners every week in an attempt to resolve issues. Oyo claims that despite partner issues, its partner base has grown 30-40 per cent in India last year, and currently stands at nearly 20,000 across different cities.

Over the past one year, the start-up has also been actively engaged in launching new programmes - OPEN (Oyo partner engagement network) and Sambandh - to stem the growing discontent in the partner community. It has recently opened its first partner support center in Gurgaon, where partners can walk in if they have any issues. More such centers are planned to be opened in other cities.

The 'Soft' Corner

Recently, in an interview, Agarwal said that merely putting superstar Marilyn Monroe's posters in some hotels improved the RevPARs in the US. While Monroe might be adding to Oyo's fortunes, SoftBank is perhaps spoiling it.

No matter how much Agarwal tries to downplay SoftBank's influence on Oyo, recent events hint at growing control of Masayoshi Son, the founder of SoftBank. Son's authority is not just evident in Oyo's business strategy but also in the way he seems to be using the company for his mega $97-billion Vision Fund.

Son's strategy is to fund investee companies with a minimum of $100 million, drive them to becoming market leaders, and then list them. It seems a similar model is being attempted at Oyo, too - expand in different geographies, turn profitable and go for public listing.

However, in October, when Oyo announced a fresh round of funding of $1.5 billion, it raised questions on SoftBank's influence at Oyo. A part of this funding - $700 million - was infused by Agarwal to hike his stake in the start-up. That's not all. Agarwal has plans to purchase Oyo's shares worth $2 billion, which would increase his shareholding from 9 per cent to about 26 per cent.

While the company had said the funds raised in the last round would be used to expand in the US, and grow the vacation rental business in Europe, in reality, it is largely a matter of shares changing hands between the existing shareholders. And in the process, the transaction added another $5 billion to the Oyo's valuation. Added to that is the fact that Agarwal's $700 million comes in the form of loans from Japanese financial groups such as Mizuho, Nomura Holdings and one unidentified bank, all of which have deep links with SoftBank.

These moves are in stark contrast to what Agarwal had told BT last year about his shareholding reducing. "I have diluted my holding but I have no regrets. I feel that I have the opportunity to make such a big difference, which is what inspired me in the first place to start it," he had said.

SoftBank's Vision Fund, which is under fire for the WeWork debacle and the poor Uber IPO, reported its first-ever quarterly loss of $8.9 billion in 14 years in the September quarter followed by $2 billion loss in the December 2019 quarter. "Oyo's lofty valuation has helped SoftBank. Pinning hopes on Oyo is obvious after two of its big investments came a cropper," says a VC founder.

"SoftBank was backing Oyo blindly. But Son is in a jam, and that's why there was a need for restructuring. Now, suddenly, SoftBank is unable to raise another $100 billion for Vision Fund-II. Oyo's metrics are wrong. All these start-ups grew in the era of gross merchandise value. Nobody thought about unit economics, sustainability, and profitability. Oyo is no longer a tech play. That was also the biggest problem with WeWork. The public market said that this is not a tech company but a real estate business. They were borrowing assets for the long term, and selling it on short-term leases. There was this luster and glamor of SoftBank. WeWork has sorted out everything," says a mid-scale hotel promoter quoted above.

US-based co-working giant WeWork was one of the largest investments of SoftBank. Last year, when WeWork tried to list on Nasdaq, its valuation tanked from $47 billion to less than $5 billion in a matter of weeks as investors got spooked over its flawed business model. As a result, SoftBank had to take a severe beating on that investment, and orchestrate a $9-billion bailout.

"They [SoftBank] are the largest shareholder. We operate like a Board-run company. There's a perception out there that SoftBank is sending instructions to Oyo; that's completely untrue. It's like any other company where you continuously engage," explains Oyo's Kapoor.

The other part of the valuation puzzle is its diversification into other verticals such as co-working, co-living, student housing, and weddings. Experts say the idea is to confuse investors as it is difficult to value each vertical separately and arrive at a fair number. If the company was just in hotels, it would be easier to value the company accurately.

Oyo, however, maintains that all these verticals are fast-growing segments. "The wedding business has upside. The demographic trends in India are so favorable to it, and there's no organized player of our size and scale. The co-living business is a strong growth area too. Thirty-five million people move cities every year - either for first and second jobs or for studies. That's a large population that is not going to buy houses. Our job is to take care of partners and keep the equilibrium going? It is never perfect," says Kapoor.

What's Next ?

It is now clear that if Oyo has to survive, it needs to focus on profit-making businesses. The unprofitable segments have to be either shut down or their formats changed. The future of Oyo largely depends on its ability to turn profitable, and hopefully list on bourses in future. But that's going to be a long journey with several imponderables.

One of the 'ifs' is Oyo's $10-billion valuation, which holds water in just two instances. One is if the company goes public or if a third-party buys it. "If Marriott or Accor or Hilton buys Oyo, I would be extremely surprised. These companies like the growth story but not the quality and they will not want to be associated with that. Look at Accor, which bought OneFineStay, which was the upper end of the Airbnb model; it's suffered a setback," says a hotelier.

The IPO route seems to be the only possible option.

"The restructuring at Oyo is a step in the right direction. Exponential growth always leads to some collateral damage and it was inevitable that Oyo would need to course-correct. Given where it is in its life cycle, Oyo needs to raise the next round of funding from capital markets, for which it requires better operating capabilities for analysts to find favor with the stock," says HVS Anarock's Lamba.

While there are companies that have gone for an IPO in the US and China without being profitable, regulations in India are typically strict for listing.

Apart from that, "in India, there are credibility issues with someone like Oyo. SoftBank will make them go for an IPO somewhere else. With WeWork, they were not able to build the book, and the IPO crashed. Will there be buyers for Oyo? I don't know," says Hotelivate's Thadani.

For now, Agarwal's mission has hit a speed breaker. Nobody said his journey would be easy, but nobody had thought that it would be puzzling either. Setting things in order could be Agarwal's key to solving the Oyo puzzle.

OYO BOARDS OF DIRECTORS

Name	Type	Representing	Status	Duration
Ritesh Agarwal	Team	-	Current	11y 9m
Bejul Somaia	Investor	Lightspeed Venture Partners	Current	8y 7m
Ashish Agrawal	Investor	-	Past	4y 7m
Gautam Mago	Investor	Sequoia Capital	Past	3y 3m
Justin Wilson	Investor	SoftBank Capital	Past	2y 3m
Min Zhang	Investor	Huazhuhui	Past	2y 5m
Mohit Bhatnagar	Investor	Sequoia Capital	Past	2y 5m
Munish Ravinder Varma	Investor	SoftBank Vision Fund	Past	3y 2m
Neil Mehta	Investor	Greenoaks	Past	4y 0m
Abhishek Gupta	Independent board member	-	Current	5y 6m
Aditya Ghosh	Independent board member	-	Current	4y 0m

Deepa Bikaramnsingh Malik	Independent board member	-	Current	2y 2m
Steve Albrecht	Independent board member	-	Current	3y 7m
Troy Alstead	Independent board member	-	Current	2y 2m
William Steve Albrecht	Independent board member	-	Current	3y 7m
Amit Kumar	Independent board member	-	Past	0y 1m
Betsy Atkins	Independent board member	-	Past	1y 10m
Gerardo Isaac Lopez	Independent board member	-	Past	1y 7m
Mark Schwartz	Independent board member	-	Past	0y 6m

OYO FUNDINGS

Oyo has 17 funding rounds where 3 Seed , 2 Early-Stage , 11 Late-Stage , 1 Debt total funding oyo got $3.24B with Investors 69 (55 Institutional , 14 Angels).

and the largest funding is $1.5B.

Q- How much funding did OYO raise in its latest funding round?

OYO raised $5M in its latest funding round, which was Series F round held on Aug 20, 2021.

Q- How much funding has OYO raised till date?

OYO has raised a total funding of $3.24B over 17 rounds.

List of all funding rounds of OYO

Date of funding	Funding Amount	Round Name	Post money valuation	Revenue multiple	Investors
Aug 20, 2021	$5M	Series F	$11.2B	20.0x	Microsoft
Jul 16, 2021	$660M	Conventional Debt	-	-	Fidelity Investments
Mar 01, 2021	Undisclosed	Series F	$9.76B	-	GSV
Jan 06, 2021	$7.4M	Series F	$9.76B	12.0x	Hindustan Media Ventures
Oct 07, 2019	$1.5B	Series F	-	-	SoftBank Vision Fund, SoftBank Group, Airbnb, Peak XV Partners, Ra Hospitality, Lightspeed India
Mar 27, 2019	$74.4M	Series E	$4.66B	8.0x	Airbnb
Feb 14, 2019	$100M	Series E	$4.57B	9.0x	Didi
Dec 31, 2018	$100M	Series E	$4.57B	10.0x	Grab
Sep 25, 2018	$1B	Series E	-	-	SoftBank Vision Fund, Greenoaks, Airbnb, Peak XV Partners, Grab, Didi,

					Lightspeed India
Sep 13, 2017	$10M	Series D	-	-	China Lodging Holding
Sep 07, 2017	$260M	Series D	$855M	9.0x	Hero MotoCorp, SoftBank Vision Fund, Greenoaks, Huazhuhui, Peak XV Partners, Global Ivy Ventures, Sequoia Capital, China Lodging Holding, Lightspeed India
Jul 22, 2016	$61.7M	Series C	$455M	49.0x	SoftBank Vision Fund
Aug 03, 2015	$100M	Series B	$388M	187.0x	SoftBank Vision Fund, Greenoaks, Peak XV Partners, Lightspeed India
Sep 29, 2014	$25M	Series A	$21.9M	92.0x	Greenoaks, Peak XV Partners, DSG Consumer Partners, Lightspeed India

Date	Amount	Round	Valuation	Multiple	Investors
Mar 31, 2014	$671K	Seed	$2.38M	20.0x	Lightspeed India, DSG Consumer Partners, Peak XV Partners
Feb 11, 2014	$3.25K	Angel	$500K	7.0x	Sadeesh Raghavan
Nov 27, 2012	$74.3K	Seed	$417K	14.9x	DSG Consumer Partners, Lightspeed India, SGR Ventures, RAAY Global Investments, Ashok Kumar Damani, Bharat Mehta, Bharat Banka, Anand Ladsariya, Sadeesh Raghavan, Rabi Kiran Sahoo, Ashish Nandkishor Agarwal, Vinod Sood, South Yarra Holdings, Nitin Agarwal

OYO Investors

Q- Who are the lead investors in OYO's latest funding round?

Microsoft is the lead investor in OYO's latest funding round held on Aug 20, 2021.

Q- How many investors does OYO have?

- OYO has a total of 69 investors.
- 55 are institutional investors including SoftBank Vision Fund and 54 others.
- 14 are Angel investors including Sadeesh Raghavan and 13 others.

List of OYO's institutional investors

- Microsoft, located in Redmond (United States), made their first investment in OYO on Aug 20, 2021 in its Series F round.
- Fidelity Investments, located in Boston (United States), made their first investment in OYO on Jul 16, 2021 in its Conventional Debt round.
- GSV, located in Surat (India), made their first investment in OYO on Mar 01, 2021 in its Series F round.
- Hindustan Media Ventures, located in Delhi (India), made their first investment in OYO on Jan 06, 2021 in its Series F round.
- SoftBank Vision Fund, located in London (United Kingdom), made their first investment in OYO on Aug 03, 2015 in its Series B round.

- SoftBank Group, located in Minato City (Japan), made their first investment in OYO on Oct 07, 2019 in its Series F round.

- Airbnb made their first investment in OYO on Oct 07, 2019 in its Series F round.

- Peak XV Partners, located in Bengaluru (India), made their first investment in OYO on Mar 31, 2014 in its Seed round.

- Ra Hospitality, located in Bengaluru (India), made their first investment in OYO on Oct 07, 2019 in its Series F round.

- Lightspeed India, located in Bengaluru (India), made their first investment in OYO on Nov 27, 2012 in its Seed round.

- Airbnb, located in San Francisco (United States), made their first investment in OYO on Sep 25, 2018 in its Series E round.

- Didi, located in Haidian (China), made their first investment in OYO on Sep 25, 2018 in its Series E round.

- Grab, located in Singapore (Singapore), made their first investment in OYO on Sep 25, 2018 in its Series E round.

- Greenoaks, located in San Francisco (United States), made their first investment in OYO on Aug 03, 2015 in its Series B round.

- China Lodging Holding, located in Hong Kong (China), made their first investment in OYO on Sep 07, 2017 in its Series D round.

- Hero MotoCorp, located in Delhi (India), made their first investment in OYO on Sep 07, 2017 in its Series D round.

- Huazhuhui, located in Shanghai (China), made their first investment in OYO on Sep 07, 2017 in its Series D round.

- Global Ivy Ventures, located in Delhi (India), made their first investment in OYO on Sep 07, 2017 in its Series D round.

- Sequoia Capital, located in Menlo Park (United States), made their first investment in OYO on Sep 07, 2017 in its Series D round.

- Greenoaks, located in San Francisco (United States), made their first investment in OYO on Sep 29, 2014 in its Series A round.

- DSG Consumer Partners, located in Ebene City (Mauritius), made their first investment in OYO on Nov 27, 2012 in its Seed round.

- SGR Ventures, located in Mumbai (India), made their first investment in OYO on Nov 27, 2012 in its Seed round.

- RAAY Global Investments, located in Mumbai (India), made their first investment in OYO on Nov 27, 2012 in its Seed round.

- South Yarra Holdings, located in Mumbai (India), made their first investment in OYO on Nov 27, 2012 in its Seed round.

Frequently asked questions about OYO's funding and investors

Q- How many funding rounds does OYO have?

OYO has total 17 funding rounds:

- 11 Late-Stage rounds
- 3 Seed rounds
- 2 Early-Stage rounds
- 1 Debt round

Q- Which was the largest funding round of OYO?

OYO's largest funding round was a Series F round held on Oct 07, 2019 for $1.5B.

FUNDING ROUND WITH MICROSOFT

Tech giant Microsoft has invested $5 million in the Gurugram-based hospitality major Oyo, according to the filings with the Registrar of Companies (RoC). The transaction is a part of the Series F2 round of the company and puts OYO's valuation at $9.6 billion, confirmed YourStory's sources.

According to the filing with the Ministry of Corporate Affairs, OYO has allotted five equity shares and 80 preference shares to Microsoft corporation at an issue price of $58,490 per share to raise $5 million.

WHAT YOU HAVE LEARNT NOW, MAKE SOME NOTES SO THAT YOU CANNOT FORGET

CHAPTER 9
AWARDS AND ACHIEVEMENTS

ACHIEVEMENTS

- First Resident Asian to win '20 Under 20' Thiel Fellowship in 2013.
- One of the Top 50 Entrepreneurs by TATA First Dot Awards in 2013.
- One of the 8 Hottest Teenage Start-up Founders in the World by Business Insider in 2013.
- He was one of the finalists of the Global Student Entrepreneurship Awards-India
- Received TiE-Lumis Entrepreneurial Excellence Award in 2014.
- Business World Young Entrepreneur Award (2015)
- Digital Champion of the Year at Brand Excellence Awards (2015)
- Startup of the Year- Express IT Award (2015)
- Star Youth Achiever Award at 8th YOUTH MARKETING & SOCIAL MEDIA FORUM (2016)
- NDTV Dream Chaser of the Year (2016)
- Forbes 30 under 30 - Consumer Tech (2016) (Global, India, Asia)
- Fortune 40 under 40 (2016) 1

- The Economic Times 40 under 40 (2016)
- New Age Entrepreneur Award by Asian Centre for Corporate Governance & Sustainability (2016)
- OneDirect Quest CX Award for Best Use of Social Media (2016)
- No. 2 in BT Coolest Start-ups Survey 2016
- Asian Centre's New Age Entrepreneur Award (2017)
- Gaurav Samman by The Government of Haryana (2017)
- GQ India - 50 Most Influential Young Leaders (2016, 2017)
- Real Innovation Awards by London Business School - If you don't succeed at first category (2017)
- India's Most Promising Hotel Network, HolidayIQ Better Holiday Awards 2017
- Best Entrepreneur of 2018 by International Hospitality Council (IHC) (2018) 3
- StartAP Entrepreneur of the Year Award (2018)
- Forbes India Tycoons of Tomorrow (2018)
- Dataquest IT Person of the Year (2018)
- OYO topped the maiden list of LinkedIn's Top Startups in India (2018)
- Fast Company: OYO among Top 10 Most Innovative Companies in India (2018)

- Startup of the Year at The Economic Times Startup Awards (2018)
- TiE's QGlue Design-led Entrepreneurship Awards (2018)
- Best Travel Startup – Jury at Zee Business Travel Awards (2018)
- CNBC's Young Turk of the Year (2019)
- The Open Republic Achievers Awards - Business New Age category (2019)
- BTVi National Awards for Marketing Excellence: Young Achiever of the year (2019) - Ritesh Agarwal
- BTVi National Awards for Marketing Excellence: CEO of the year (2019) -Ritesh Agarwal
- Agarwal was featured in the Bloomberg 50 list as 'The Amazingly Ambitious Hotelier' (2019)
- The 50 most powerful people in India by India Today and the Tycoons of Tomorrow' by Forbes India. (2019)
- His net worth was estimated to be approximately $1 billion (7000 crore INR) according to IIFL Wealth Hurun India Rich List. (2019)
- Market Entrant of the Year 2019 (UK-India Awards)
- Fast Company's World's Most Innovative Companies for 2019 – India edition
- Best Startup – SATTE Awards 2019

- LinkedIn has recognized OYO as one of the top employee attractors in India four years in a row (2016, 2017, 2018, 2019)

- Ritesh Agarwal, Founder & Group CEO, OYO Hotels & Homes won 'The Millennial Maverick' Award at GQ & * * * * Mercedes-Benz Restless for Tomorrow Awards (2020)

- In March 2020, Ivanka Trump, the senior advisor to President Donald Trump, had lauded an initiative by OYO Hotels to offer free stays to doctors, nurses in the US helping in the fight against the novel coronavirus, describing the gesture as "impactful acts of benevolence".

- At the age of 22 he became a millionaire

- At the age of 24, his wealth was estimated at $1.1 billion (₹7,800 crore) in the Hurun Global Rich List 2020. Agarwal comes second only after cosmetics queen Kylie Jenner who has also amassed $1.1 billion at the age of 22.

WHAT YOU HAVE LEARNT NOW, MAKE SOME NOTES SO THAT YOU CANNOT FORGET

CHAPTER 10
UNCOVERED FACTS AND INTERVIEWS

UNCOVERED FACTS

- Oyo boards are inspired by Airtel boards.
- His first life-changing moment was the event that he attended the Indus Entrepreneur (tie event) At that time his age was 16 or 17.
- He used to sneak into the event of entrepreneurship. Because he doesn't have money to buy the tickets for those events.
- While traveling in his free time when he was in Kota he developed a huge hunger for solving problems in the travelling sector.
- Ritesh quit Kota to prepare SAT so that he could go to the us for his further studies but unfortunately or fortunately it never happened.
- He had founded the company when he wasn't even 20.
- He started Oravel as an Indian Airbnb.
- Ritesh was confused between startup and research he was researching ammonia.
- He failed six times before succeeding
- Before Oravel he failed max to max in 10 business like he was trying to open his travel agency, sim card selling, and so on.
- Ritesh Agarwal was not confident about his studies.

- He joined the college in Delhi and went for 2 to 3 days after that he was postponing one day for building this company oravel.
- Ritesh doubted his ability to do well in college or work for someone. Hence he jumped into something like building OYO. He says, "I knew if I had gone to college, I would not have done well. And then my family would hate me. So I felt if my family were to hate me anyway, I would rather do what I feel very excited about!"
- At some point of time he went broke and he went broke he didn't have money to pay for his house rent so his landlord threw him out.
- When he went broke he used to sell sim cards and his wife who was at that time his girlfriend helped him with some money.
- 2nd turning point of his life was when he got a chance to become a fellow with a 1 lakh dollar winning prize.
- But he failed to build it so after working on his flaws May 2013 oravel was renamed and launched as Oyo.
- It took 2 years to establish Oyo.
- Oyo has a secret co-founder Manish Sinha who joined Ritesh when Oravel Ritesh convinced Manish to sell his stake of 10% to 15 % of 28 lakh rupees and today that stake is worth more than 1000 caores.
- At the age of 21, he became the youngest millionaire.
- At the age of 26, he became the 2nd youngest billionaire in the world.

- Today, OYO is racing with speed to be one of the world's biggest hotel chains.
- At the age of 29, he became the youngest shark tank judge.
- While he has not even attained 25 years of age, Ritesh Agarwal, the CEO of OYO has seen it all – popularity, business success, and financial prosperity. He has made something unique at a time when others had not even thought of it – a hotel booking software that would assure room for anyone at their favorite hotel at competitive prices.
- Ritesh's task of convincing the VCs to fund his venture was not an easy one. When he attempted to find a solution to the hotel booking process, something like OYO had not been built earlier. The investors asked if there was anything similar to what he was trying to build. While they all interpreted his venture as a real estate business, only two months later they all started when competition started building up.
- Ritesh had once commented that he failed six times before he succeeded in his OYO venture. Ritesh says, "If you have not failed, you have not hardened yourself."

INTERVIEWS

Interview taken by CNBC-TV18 with Ritesh Agarwal and Aditya ghosh

Q- From 2013, in just six years, what a journey; and talk to us about how this is going to be the next leaf in OYO's journey?

Agarwal: Look at OYO, we have constantly said we think a few quarters or a few years ahead. So back in 2014 or 2015, when Abhinav Sinha came along, a lot of people said that for such a young company why does it need a high profile COO and eventually we all know that turned out to be for the best. When Maninder Gulati came in 2015 that was great for our organization. Same was the case last year when a lot of people said that your business essentially is India and if Aditya is a CEO of OYO India, then why are you making this decision? Our view was looking one year ahead. Today OYO India is probably 40 percent.

Now, when we think about OYO two years later, we need a fantastic partner on our board who can help think about corporate governance, about the path towards profitability, and help drive the organization in that direction. We started making these decisions a few months back, we brought in Betsy Atkins to begin with, Aditya is a great addition and we will constantly look at bringing in great quality on board to strengthen this group.

Q- On November 20, you joined as the CEO and within one year you have been elevated to the board, an incredible year. But I feel like there is a lot more that has been on behind the scenes. Talk to us about that and what

is that you think that you can offer as part of being on the board as opposed to being a CEO?

Aditya Ghosh: It has been just a phenomenal year. It has been an exhilarating experience and the way the company has grown both in South Asia as well as globally. We keep saying it is a once-in-a-lifetime opportunity and it is great to see that many of those dreams are becoming a reality. Somehow we have come across a business model that has secular need around the world. The company is growing faster than we had expected it to grow, the company is growing at a much bigger geographical reach that basically means there is more expectation from us. So again, as Ritesh said, let us look a few years ahead. What is expected of a truly global company like OYO, what kind of governance would be expected of us, what kind of board would be expected of us, how do we deliver on what we are promising to the consumer, how do we become a profitable business, how do we stay true to some of the core promises and that is where I guess the fact that we were beginning to deliver on what we had promised in South Asia and thanks to fantastic team that I have around me, I think that gave us the confidence to say let us start discussing about what tomorrow and day after and a week after that is going to look like.

I have spent the last 15 years running a large consumer business. I have had the privilege of running a publicly traded company which is a large business, a profitable business. But most importantly, being deeply immersed in OYO for the last one year has brought an experience that I hope that I can now take to the board. We have got a great board. We have got very experienced industrial directors, we have got an independent director like Betsy, we have got a founder like Ritesh and I hope I can bring that management experience depth into that board and say - look now let us start again putting together the building blocks which will - I don't know how to put it - may be a dream of being seen not just as the largest and the fastest, but one of the most well-respected 'blue-chip' companies, I think that is the dream.

Q- I was listening to what you were saying very carefully and one thing that you said was there are a lot of expectations from OYO. While there are expectations from the industry, while there are expectations that you guys have for yourselves, I believe that the expectations of investors have also risen and if we can put it this way, SoftBank is suddenly now looking at India to fulfill their IPO dream. So tell me as candidly as possible, everything that went down with a company like WeWork and then SoftBank is now probably looking at OYO to kind of fulfill that dream and go IPO. Do you as founder and CEO of the company and now board members feel the heat of that?

Agarwal: Generally, it is important to make sure that you can disassociate the sentiment with the fact. For us, SoftBank Vision Fund has been a great partner as has been well articulated. We have always been expected to just deliver the plan. We had a business plan that we said out, a couple of years back, and our shareholders including Vision Fund just expect us to get there. Specifically about IPO and the public offering, as you may know, our balance sheet is upwards of $2 billion.

Revenues are up by 4x but losses are up by 6x as well?

Agarwal: So those numbers are not an audited financial yet, so please expect our financials to come soon, but even if you assume that that is close to $300 million. The past few years combined is probably a little bit more versus that the balance sheet is very strong, so there is no reason to try and be public immediately. Our focus is on the business, building a good company and at the same time we are building the right kind of organization like Aditya says to be IPO ready. Then when we make the choice in terms of a company, it is the decision of the board and we have a fantastic board including our new incoming board member.

Q- This is why I am asking, is there more pressure to go public from SoftBank at this point?

Aditya Ghosh: No. When you step back – I keep saying that the initial public offering is a milestone in a journey. You cannot time a milestone but you have to be ready for that milestone.

So it is not pressure but it is not an unreasonable expectation from a board-run company like OYO where the management team and the board are expected to say, are you building a business that as Ritesh was saying, I kept saying – should it be IPO ready? So that when the circumstances arrive, when the board comes together and says now is the time to push the button on a publicly traded business, then the business should not hold it back.

What that means is – is it a profitable business, is it a proven business model, is there a great future to it? An IPO is only a trigger point where you now have a bigger expectation of even more shareholders. Therefore, we will focus on building this credible business.

As and when the board decides, we will hopefully be ready with a business that is well-placed, well-respected and then you can take it.

Q- But overall, everything that happened with WeWork has no consequences on you guys?

Agarwal: I think that is a different question altogether but an important question.

To begin with, I think it is very hard to deny that WeWork changed the way people went to work and we respect them for that. However, every global event like that of WeWork is an important learning experience for all the large scale start-ups and young companies and one of the things that is clearly being seen in the ecosystem is that high growth only is not appreciated, growth with high focus on profitability is accepted. That is something that we fully acknowledge and the best way to be able to think about it is sort of saying how OYO, in its view, looks at that specific feedback that it is being received for, broadly every high-growth company. Here at OYO, we feel we have mature geographies and we have new geographies.

Mature geographies are like the geographies that my colleague like Aditya has been driving or on the other hand new geography was China last year. This year, it is the United States or Europe. So whenever we bring mature geographies, there should be a consistent improvement in underlying economics.

Our audited statements have not been filed yet but very soon, we will have our audited statements and annual reports published and you can expect a perspective about how our mature businesses are continuously showing the path for newer businesses to be able to show significant operating efficiencies.

Last but not the least, OYO has built a reasonably large business. If you look at our revenues, scale, etc., of course until last year, the current year numbers will be out hopefully very soon. If you look at those metrics, you will realize that for a company of this size, the amount of capital we have consumed among the young start-up ecosystem, it is not very low but at the same time, it is not dramatically higher than what a lot of other companies in the ecosystem had generally seen and will continue to try to be more capital efficient as an organization.

Q- It is interesting you have said that because we have been tracking the OYO story right here on CNBC-TV18. I personally had an opportunity to speak with you and the one word we would hear all the time from you is growth, growth, growth. However, it is interesting that for the past few months or at least a year we are hearing more words being added in, which is profitability, corporate governance and sustainable business. These are words that we didn't hear as part of the OYO narrative for the longest time. Is it fair to say that it is not purely because the company is maturing or is there a different agenda that has been set in place now?

Aditya Ghosh: I think the company is evolving and as the company evolves, when you are starting up, when I talked to many early-stage companies - and I don't think we are an early-stage company anymore - but when I talked to young founders the first thing that always comes up and the question that comes up is how do you scale up, how do you grow up.

Clearly, this business model has been able to prove that we have passed that. Then last year, Ritesh started putting together the building blocks saying, how do we now put in all the other ambitions which come into play. So I think this is just an evolution.

Q- What I want to ask you is, is this change in narrative organic or was it a shift overnight or something that triggered the thing, we need to focus more on corporate governance, we need to focus more on profitability, we need to focus on the fact that we have to build and create a sustainable business?

Agarwal: It is somehow linked to the scale and the aspiration. When we were a reasonably large Indian business, we started saying India needs to have high-quality corporate governance leadership and as a part of that was Aditya coming as a leader of the India business.

Now with our expansion worldwide and the scale of performance that we are seeing, we feel that breadth today doesn't give as much upside as much as depth and as we keep going deeper in the geographies that we are already in, the immediate question that gets asked is, as you go deeper, operating efficiencies and hence sustainability and path to profitability will come but when you do that at such large scale, doing it in the right way is extremely valuable due to which corporate governance becomes valuable.

So in my view, this is a part of growing up for the company and this has been the case for the last few months. As you said, it has been – I feel that around May or June a lot of these discussions started and it is a happy feeling. Especially for me as an entrepreneur; in 2013 the question was will you survive the next week or not. It is a good evolution to move from being next week to do I survive or do I have to go back to university. It has been a significant revolution and I am very thankful to have this opportunity.

Q- What can we expect now from the grown-up version of OYO and especially with this change in movement and Rohit being elevated as the CEO of OYO and you being part of the board, what is the next couple of months going to look like?

Aditya Ghosh: I think we have some immediate priorities. The immediate priority is to make sure that Rohit and I work alongside together to make sure that the business consolidates and comes together under a new leadership, which is Rohit. The good news is that – I am still going to be based in Gurgaon and I am right here and I am available to the team as well as Rohit for anytime that they need to make sure that we transition it well. Even right now, my current boss is going to expect me to deliver on my December targets.

But the third is how do we start thinking about what the next money is going to look like, how do we build global capabilities and that is not just me, there are a lot of leaders out here who are now playing global roles and how do we bring that together because the sweet spot of success will be when we are able to transport these pockets of excellence into a replica which can be replicated all around the world and this whole organization – there are different parts and different stages to it but the whole organization – hopefully one year from now, you will come back and say yes, you talked about some of this stuff last winter and yes, you have come good.

Agarwal: But maybe next year you would be saying that, alright, you did some of these things right but why are you not growing.

Q- You pre-empted my next question. I want to now focus on the human level of running a business. You started the company, OYO was your dream-child and just within a few years it became much bigger than – I don't know if you have anticipated it to grow at this scale, there were new folks who came and who took charge and stepped up when needed and now are partners in making this dream come true, how does that work on the human level, especially right now when we were talking about. Aditya came in as the CEO, so it takes some time to get used to that transition and now very soon this CEO-board member relationship is going to transition into co-board members.

Aditya Ghosh: One common thing, whenever Ritesh and I get together - and I was telling one of my colleagues just a short while ago – we have this uncanny habit, whenever we get together if we have planned an hour, it will be seven hours and we always end up missing meals and one of the other is saying aren't you hungry, that is a very common thing. Obviously we have a lot to talk about all the time.

Q- What I am trying to understand is that apart from skipping meals together, what is it that you guys have to do to get used to that transition to get used to that change in organizational structure because that dynamic is much deeper than what it looks like from the outside ?

Agarwal: That is the whole perspective. At the outside, it feels like a much more complicated dynamic but for us here in the inside the way we think about it is that all of us came here with a common goal that is how do we build OYO into a successful company and this is related to the previous question you shared as well that we will all be available to make sure whatever is required to make OYO more successful, which is why it becomes very easy for me to be able to make these decisions and same for all our other leaders possibly because all of us say that we came here because we saw a dream that what OYO could be in the years to come.

Q- You don't feel possessive about the company - the company that you have built and is now driven by so many board members and so many people?

Agarwal: I never feel that I built the company and I want to be very honest in saying that, I am very thankful that I have the opportunity to be in the key meeting rooms and the discussions, I would happily be just a fly in the wall.

Ghosh: I feel very possessive about the company.

Agarwal: I don't. I feel that the way we think about it is saying that it is a company first and in some way OYO has been a pioneer there where we have said that in India when most companies would say that the CEO has to be the founder, I have been very happily saying that we need to bring an executive leader who can bring and make OYO more successful so that I can go pursue additional ambitions. From our perspective, at the human level, all we say is do we all fundamentally does our heart beat for the company? If the heart beats for the company, do everything that is required to make the company successful.

Interview taken by Times of India with Ritesh

Q- Have there been failures? How did you deal with them?

The reality of a startup is you have failures very often. My biggest one was when I went broke very early when I was staying in all these hotels. When you go broke, generally your first reaction is to call family, right? I could not because I was very young, and if I told my family, the first thing they would have said is, come back. As an entrepreneur, when you have such strong belief in solving a problem, there's no way you will give up.

Q- How do you cope with criticism?

I respect them and believe that constructive criticism is very valuable, and whenever questions like those have come, the best way is being honest. Now, the reality is when it's not constructive criticism, what you mention can be twisted. But I have learned to be true to yourself. On a lighter note, success is directly proportional to the criticism you get. So, at many levels, it makes you feel you are doing something right.

Q- It's been a rollercoaster ride for you. How did you get here?

Post 10th grade, I came to the northern half of the country. I realized that the usual education did not excite me at all because I felt that understanding trajectory motions in chemistry help me solve real-life problems. Every weekend I would take a train to Delhi and sneak into startup events. I really enjoyed meeting entrepreneurs who were solving big problems. They were way smarter than me. I knew this is where I had to be. (After graduating from school, Agarwal started Oravel, similar to Airbnb.)

Q- How did OYO Rooms happen? How is it different from everything out there?

We realized that the problem was predictability, the problem was enabling the right guest experiences. Hence, we decided to solve that. I picked up a hotel and spent 10 months just on that, branding and enabling a great experience. Globally, none of the hotels enable the entire process of checking in and checking out through a mobile app. Every check that happens at OYO, happens via a tablet and that is very similar to what the drivers of Ola use.

I know what time a customer checked in, what he ordered, did it get delivered on time, did he order for sling bags, and so on. And when the customer checks out, he can walk out like how you get out of cabs because if you have a wallet it's completely hassle-free.

Whenever I think of OYO's vision, it's about solving the problem and also ensuring an awesome experience. Average time taken to book an OYO room is 4 seconds using our app. Average time taken by any online marketplace is one day or more. It's as hassle-free as being in your home; nobody asks for an identity card when you get into your home. In the future, you can actually give away houses, you don't need to own houses. Our vision is that in five years, you should have your own house, and everything else should be an OYO room—no relative homes, no friend's place.

Q- What advantages and disadvantages do young founders have? Do we put undue premium on being young?

I don't think so. If anything, younger people might find it tougher to just go out and pitch an idea and start negotiating..Then again, kids are getting smarter and more confident by the day. On the other hand, older folks may find it tougher to let go of their comfort zones.So, really, age is just a number.

CATEGORY LEADER

RITESH AGARWAL founded Oravel in 2011 when he was 17	among others
	Has **40,000 rooms** across **160 cities** on its platform
Oravel Stays was a platform to list & book budget hotels	
	Claims to be clocking **25,000 booked** room-nights a day (**0.75 million** a month)
Pivoted and became Oyo Rooms in 2013	
Has raised **$125 million** from investors like Softbank, Lighspeed Venture Partners, Sequoia Capital	Competes with Zo Rooms, Stayzilla, Treebo, Fab Hotels as well as Golbibo, MakeMyTrip & others

Q- You've said openly that you encourage students to drop out of college, just like you did. Why?

I don't dissuade people from formal education. What I encourage them to do is to follow their dreams. I don't subscribe to a curriculum-driven education that has no space for students to build on their ideas.In our education system, we're so focused on the building blocks that sometimes we try to keep the kids from looking at the larger picture I'm not saying either is bad – just that if someone is ready to paint on a bigger canvas, education should prepare him, support him and not hold him back.

Q- Coming to Oyo Rooms, are you a brand or simply an aggregation platform for hotels? How are you addressing

the cash burn issues; is consolidation in your sector on the cards?

We have worked hard to be recognized as a brand that offers predictable, affordable and standardized accommodation to travelers. The market potential in the hospitality industry is huge and we are well-poised to capitalize on it. Consolidation or not, the scale of this business will drive up profitability for market leaders. We have a strong operations focus. We have executed well, and have strong unit economics. So we are confident of how the business will shape up.

Q- Many startups in India are currently being built on the support of constant capital infusion.

But with markets turning, founders are being forced to change course. Having been a part of this boom cycle, how do you see the ecosystem evolving from here on?

I think companies with solid business fundamentals and focus on strong unit economics will not be impacted as much as those that were burning cash to gain market-share or notch up customers. We expect to see some rationalization. Things are likely to get tougher for companies that are not category-leaders.

Ritesh Agarwal opens up about job losses, Aditya Ghosh, governance issues, and SoftBank's role

Q- : What went wrong with Oyo? There have been job losses, allegations that Aditya Ghosh is on his way out and about fake inventory, among other things.

Agarwal: I want to address each of these issues separately.

Specific to restructuring, we have operated with a fairly straightforward perspective. We build business with a long term view, reflect upon what went right, and what did not go right. Whenever we do something right, we keep doubling down. Whenever there is something, which can be improved, we reflect and ensure we make improvements.

As a part of this process, Oyo did see that as we had grown rapidly in 2019, we had presence in over 80 countries, revenue grew multi-fold, margins improved. This is good news, but it was time to reflect upon what could be improved.

In a few specific organizations (inside Oyo) it was important to resize the organization to continue to grow rapidly. Organizations tend to delay change, or do the same thing repeatedly over a long period of time. We believe that it is good for Oyo and its team members for this to happen one time. This is a one-time exercise and most of it has been completed, and the remaining will happen over the next couple of weeks.

Q- : Why was this restructuring required? Why were those employees hired in the first place, and why do they need to go now?

Agarwal: We have always acquired high-quality talent. This is the first time a major restructuring is happening at Oyo. We had two-three important learnings.

The first one is sustainable growth. For the first time we realized that there are specific suburban clusters we should invest more in, and there are clusters we need to invest less in. The restructuring was a result of that realization.

Second, how do we build stronger customer trust? There were teams focusing on servicing and our partners were field based. We are centralizing our teams.

Third, as Oyo has grown in multiple parts of the world, we believe that now we have sufficient technology and infrastructure to centralize roles to build shared services.

Three of these have two perspectives in common. The first one: the organization grew as a large global company. And with scale, we learnt about some of these potential areas where we had gotten a little ahead of ourselves, and had to restructure.

Q- : So, will you do more hiring, and in which areas?

Agarwal: The new hiring will be more focussed on engineering, design, software and data science, in the future. But, in the new future we would like to stabilize the organization, and get to the outcome and plan of 2020.

Q- : How do you plan to stabilize the organization? There are so many aspects to consider: cultural, governance, unit economics and more.

Agarwal: On the culture side, Oyo has gotten here because of its team members. I have personally visited clusters and done townhalls, and explained our plans.

On the supply side, we have brought in 100 hotels in the month of January that had either left us or were asked to leave for various reasons.

In China, we have ensured that we have brought in 8,500 rooms in that context.

We are able to bring back our partners.

In the US, in the fourth week of January we signed more rooms than we have ever signed. We are able to see that people are understanding this.

But, a good company is not built on a month or two months of success. This has to be a consistent effort.

Q- : What about gross margins?

Agarwal: We are seeing an increase in gross margins, because of better site selection, and are making sure that our contracts are very seamless with our partners, so that we can make our fare share. Our gross margins have trended between 15–25 percent. We will announce our financials shortly, where you will see our revenue and EBITDA.

Q- : Will it be better than last year?

Agarwal: Markets where we are in our first year of launch are our cost markets because you have to hire the team and properties, and from the second year onwards the EBITDA keeps improving.

On a year-on-year basis the mature markets will continue to improve.

Q- : How do you manage better governance at Oyo?

Agarwal: Oyo brought in an independent director on board, Betsy Atkins. Betsy has been an investor in Yahoo, Ebay, and has been on the boards of some of the most successful American companies, like Volvo, Nasdaq, and Baja Corporation. Gerry Lopez joins us on the board as well. Gerry was the CEO of 'Extended Stay America', an extended stay hotel brand in the US.

Q- : Speaking of the board, is Aditya Ghosh moving on, as some news reports suggest?

Agarwal: Aditya is a fantastic leader, and we have worked together for a full year. He has been extremely valuable to the organization at various levels, which involves his consistent presumption of safety and security, his ability to bring new age revenue management systems, and various other efforts.

Due to this, we believe that Aditya's value to Oyo can be further expanded from India to becoming a global organisation. Aditya is not supporting Oyo passively, but he is supporting Oyo actively.

He joined our board meeting just a couple of weeks ago.

Q- : But reports suggest that Aditya doesn't come to office.

Agarwal: Oyo has six offices in Gurgaon. Aditya comes to one of the offices, so the ex-employee who commented must be talking about their office.

Q- : How important is governance for you? This is a question that is being raised on all SoftBank companies, including Oyo.

Agarwal: For me and my team, governance is an absolute must. There are three important parts to it. The first one is, and we have always taken market leadership in that, in bringing in independent directors.

Second: ensuring that the founder doesn't sell shares. I have never sold a single share of mine in the company. I have rather invested more capital in the company.

Third: making sure that a large amount of decisions are board driven in the company. It is important to have a management, which is broad-based. If you see Oyo beyond Ritesh, there is a strong team of leaders who know their organizations and can drive the results.

Q- : Oyo has been written off multiple times, and now it is being compared to WeWork.

Agarwal: Our company has grown with a great amount of attention around itself. Every time this has happened, we have only become better with it. It is very easy to say, "he says, she says" and claim that these allegations are true or untrue. We make sure we over communicate, like we are doing here. But, instead of getting bogged down, we take the learnings from those and try to improve. Because no company is perfect. Oyo is not perfect, no company is. We want to make sure we make Oyo a better company every day.

Q- : Is Oyo here to stay?

Agarwal: We have created a lot of value. In India, if you wanted to stay in a good quality hotel in Mumbai for less than Rs 2,000, it was almost impossible to do before Oyo came. If you wanted to stay at a place, which is of good quality, at the right price point in South East Asia, if you wanted a room in Europe for 100 EUR a night, these are all services that consumers really appreciate. Oyo served 40 million families last year, and that's growing as we speak.

Q- : There are allegations that there is fake inventory on Oyo. What are you doing about that?

Agarwal: We are subject to significant amounts of audit as an organization. Oyo continuously audits, not just specific operation metrics, but also financial metrics, by world class organisations.

Customer experience is very important for Oyo. 99.5 percent of our customers have a seamless experience with Oyo. But, 0.5 percent is a very bad statistic, and we are working upon that.

We will build check-in as a delight, and that will be communicated to hotels on our Oyo app. We are experimenting with that feature with a smaller group of customers right now.

Q- : Do you have pressure from SoftBank to become a profitable organization?

Agarwal: Oyo is a management-driven company. The management drives the company with board oversight. Oyo had submitted the business plan to the board of directors some time back. Our board's opinion is that we consistently deliver and that we shouldn't get distracted. There is no change that our company has seen in the last few months, depending on what has happened.

WHAT YOU HAVE LEARNT NOW, MAKE SOME NOTES SO THAT YOU CANNOT FORGET

CHAPTER 11
SPEECHLESS SPEECH

In this speech all the words are directly spoken by ritesh agarwal, the most inspiring speech i have ever heard from ritesh believe me guys just read each word of this speech you will definitely get inspired by this speech. If this can't work for you then nothing can inspire you. I am not saying that you have to complete this chapter by anyhow.

For all of you guys I have distributed his speech according to numbers so that when you feel low or when you want some motivation you just open this chapter and start reading any of the story.

From now on, Ritesh is taking the lead, enjoying and having some fun.

Let's begin ……..

In my short experience I learnt one very important thing.

"Life presents you with 2 opportunities or 2 options at all certain points of time, not 4 a,b,c,d like kaun banega crorepati, just 2 either risk or on the other hand regret."

I have always learned that whenever life presents you with either of these opportunities, taking a risk is always better than regretting not taking that risk many years from now.

So what I want to talk about is that

why risking is better than being regretful in life.

1st story

"Going after what you really really want to do"

You know all of us are in our 20's all of you are in your early 20's which means that you have very limited liabilities in life.

- You don't have a husband or wife waiting for you back home.
- You don't kid's whom you have to leave for school.

You don't have any of those pains, all you have is the ability to dream and go out and make an impact.

So in the next few years you would see some of your friends getting better ctc's / Cgpa but you really enjoying doing something else. It's okay to let that be and not be the top ctc / Cgpa candidate.

You will see some of your friends taking world trips on your facebook account and then you would feel i am having to work 16 hours a day because of my passion you would have a lot of these sacrificial feelings every week remember in the long term it will all be worth it.

Right after my 12th. 11th grade actually i had the opportunity of being so ambitious about entrepreneurship i used to read about entrepreneurs everyday there were 2 companies i was inspired by

1) Royal enfield
2) Indigo airlines

So i used to take weekend trains from kota to delhi to come and listen to those entrepreneurs most of the people around me said on weekends life is so good and you end up going every weekend to listen to entrepreneurs whom we don't even know about about then i lived in a barsati for a year in delhi and work from there to build really really small businesses most of them pretty insignificant we do more business in like one street in any street of india then what i would have. what would be my highest business at that point of time those sacrifices will all worth it because i genuinely genuinely wanted to make a difference around my self which means that if each one of us have an ambition or we learn what we have an ambition about it's okay to sacrifice the usual excitement in life for the next few years to do what you want to do. which means it is okay to take a risk being regretful of not doing what you wanted to do and **30 years later being at a bar and telling your friends you know you see this friend of mine who has done so well in his life i would have also like him if i have taken a risk you don't want to be regretful like that you want to be the person in the photo who is being talked about.**

2nt story

" Living a very happy and ambitious life but with a lot of discipline "

Right after I decided that I wanted to be an entrepreneur I used to read online about tech branches , economic times and so on about entrepreneurs and I felt what easy things it would be. You just choose a good idea and if you are intelligent enough it should just become successful. I was up for a reality check.

- When show up for meeting 10 minute late people judge you
- When you are not prepared before a conversation people would judge you

and that would happen literally every hour of the day for 365 days multiplied by the years that is the struggle we would all go through before we start something really really successful. All this period required you to put a significant amount of discipline.

I am very lucky to have 11 core cxo's in india and of course 5 more in china. There are people who come from,who are the top guys at Pcg , mckinsey and so on partnering with me. so every monday morning we all meet together and we discuss about :

- What going on business
- What are the challenges

And so on ....

I start preparing on sunday morning to make sure that next day when i go and talk about :

- The area of opportunity
- The areas that are challenges

And so on ....

I can continue earning the respect of all my colleagues to make sure that they continue to believe that I am the right person to lead the company. that is just 1% of the amount of discipline and hardwork that we would all have to go through in our lives if we believe that is a big outcome at the end of the day, which means that long term that is that risk of making sure that weekends and those evenings you could have had a better time. i am not asking you to stop them you should have a great time but when you are working putten all the efforts and discipline that you can behind it so you don't have to regret later that is my early years i could have work harder and i could have being the best person in the field that i started working on.

3rd story

"Travel as much as you can ,,

I know my parents are here. A lot of parents would say that abhi naukri lag gayi toh 2 saal baad gaadi aur 5 saal baad ghar toh lena hi chahiye. if in this period of time. you can save a little and spend on travel voh 5 saal ka 6 saal agar ho jata hai it doesn't hurt. sorry parents i would genuinely hope it in 5 years but that travel will be worth it i have learnt whatever i have learnt in my short life by means of traveling across the world. i was born and brought up in the odisha andhra pradesh border in a place where 80 % population is below poverty line so for me that was all the place that i knew about. The first time when I came to Kota I felt that the world was much broader. When I came to Delhi the world became even larger and then for 3 months everyday I stayed in a new bread and breakfast, new hotels and so on.Which got me thinking that this is so exciting.

The world over every hotel chain is 100 rooms or larger (100 kamree ke hotel chain yaa usse bade hote hai) but worldwide 95% of the hotels are 100 rooms or smaller.

So I wondered why nobody is opening the hotel chain which is 100 rooms and smaller because there are so many of them then i felt there there could be either of 2 reasons :

1) This is an idea that so many people have tried and failed in. I am probably the 1000th guy doing it.

2) This is something that nobody is seeing and probably I am the first guy seeing it so I should go to it immediately.

As an entrepreneur you are designed to be an optimist you always see a positive in anything around you. I saw the positive that at most I am going to fail and if I fail it's okay. I am still young and I have very little liabilities in life that come about because for 3 months everyday i stayed in the new breads and breakfast , hotels and so on. After that when I started the company and I had just one hotel I had the opportunity to be a thiel fellow.

When I was there for the first time in California I saw how big and ambitious people were here. i was always told by my father that if you are able to earn more salary than me. You have done very well in your life but there were people thinking about how to make the lives of millions and billions of people across the world better. There were people thinking about innovations and how to create new things that make a difference in people's lives.

All of these things that i have learnt inspired me to say even if we are building a company here in gurgaon it doesn't mean that we cannot dream to build the world largest hotel chain.

The point I'm trying to make about these ambitions , these learnings and the mistakes that you make all of this comes because you see the world in a different view than just one city or one place.

So whenever you get an opportunity to travel from the smallest villages in India to the biggest cities in the world.

kabhi bhi mauka mile please take that hands down even if that means that you might miss an important meeting or so on. I know all of you guys are bright enough to manage some of them but the amount of learnings that travel brings is incredible.

4th story

"Surrounding yourself with incredible people"

I had started oyo come back to India and we were trying to grow that company. we had one hotel in 2014 aur woh 5 mahine (months) tk ek hi hotel chl raha rahi thi. I was working very hard everyday but nothing was moving and here I was working hard. As an entrepreneur You are designed to try and control everything right. You try to say that I want everything perfect so I will control it. I used to try and do the same.

- I used to pick up phones at the call center
- I used to write accounts on telly and so on

One of us angel investor Bejul Somaia from light speed. He invites me to have lunch with him every month so I went to have lunch with him and our office was in Sohna road at that point of time and right beside that was haldiram's. The best food I used to have was haldiram's. For me the reason why this lunch used to be great is a Bejul's office in a fancy hotel. He used to always treat me to great lunches.

Meeting him was of course important but more important was a great lunch so he fed me good food after the feeding was done or after the food was done he asked me ritesh. I heard that you have been spending a lot of time on calls and with customers.

I said absolutely I love doing it. That I can do all my life he said that's perfect so we now have the head of the call center of oyo let us now recrute the CEO and I of course got the message (means ritesh understood that what Bejul was trying to say) saying it's my job to bring solid leaders and entrepreneurs in the company.

Who can build the company one level ahead of me? so that oyo outgrows one individual and becomes an institution with strong leaders. it is hard because you have to give away always but the same time you need to make sure that you bring peoples smarter than you :

- People who are going to challenge you
- People who are going to be honest with you

So one of the earliest people who then joined was Abhinav.

Abhinav was :

- The best guys at harvard business school
- Principal at BCG (boston consulting group)
- Before that ran the largest factory for ITC india

And he came and partnered with me for 1 year. and that 1 year was fabulous. We grew from one hotel to 1000 hotels. That was the biggest growth our company has seen till date in its history just because Abhinav came, Kavikrut came , Ayush came , Shreerang came.

So there was a large group of people

All very very established but they all believed in the mission that we were going after that a common man can also expect good quality living space.

I believe in all of your lives you will always have options of surrounding yourself with people who can help you get better in life they will be smarter than you hence they will challenge you to think better vs you will have people who will take you behind in life there will be people who make you feel that you are the smartest person in the room always choose to be with the formal people around yourself because you are always the average of 10 people around you. your average will only improve if the people around you are smarter and brighter than you.

So always try to get better people around yourselves that will ensure that you grow faster in life.

5th story

"Always drive for excellence never be okay by being number - 2 and it does not mean number - 1 in academics only you can choose what direction or what segment you want to be number - 1 in "

It doesn't matter what you choose to be:

- You might want to be the smartest number 1 martial arts guy
- You might be very good in academics
- You might be very good in speaking

- You might be very good in sports
- You might be the best for family
- You might be the best father in your entire generation

It's okay but

Whatever you choose to be, please always try to strive for excellence Because when you strive for excellence the amount of happiness that gives you is incredible.

Personally, for me, 2 years after building Oyo a lot of people told me that Ritesh has built a company with thousands of hotels already. Why don't you sell the company or a part of your company, take some money, and have a happier life.

And then I went back and I thought when I am 40 years or 50 years old what will make me happy will I be happy building something where you land at any part of the world , any city , town across the world and you walk out the railway station or the airport and you see an oyo signage and I point it and say I build this company or would I be happy if I was the person who made some money earlier in my life.

The answer was straight forward. I am much happier being the former who did something impactful in my life rather than the person who had more money than myself.

That is the strive for excellence that I request all of you to have because that will make sure that you are always proud of the risk you took Vs being regretful of the things you left on the table.

HEARTWARMING ENDING MESSAGE FROM RITESH

I will end it with just one thing all of us will get opportunities in our lives special opportunities but whenever you get them you should go for it and you should be prepared for it.

For many years I have continued to strive hard to build the company. There were 2 or 3 times I got the great opportunities, probably 4 I took them 2 or 3 times and I still regret that I did not take that one time that I could have.

For example : our company had

3 years back we were a small company but we already had 200 crores on the balance sheet. We had sales of close to a thousand crores when a person called Nikesh Arora called us and said, "I want to see you. Nikesh used to be head of a soft bank at that point of time so I went to meet him and he wanted to invest 600 more crores in the company so I felt we didn't need this capital and diluting my ownership now would not be the most intelligent business decision to make.

But then internally all of the management met and i thought to myself that people like Nikesh and more importantly somebody like masayoshi son who had built such large impactful companies like softbanks.

If I get the opportunity to have them on a roster of shareholders, I have the opportunity to meet them.

I can dream of making a much bigger company than I could have thought earlier so even if economically not the best decision we still choose to have a soft bank as a shareholder I look back and I feel it was one of the best decisions I made.

So when presented with an opportunity, always be ready to take it, and never take 2 steps behind saying.

- I don't know whether I can do it whether I can't do it
- Whether I can deliver or not deliver

You should have the self - confidence and believe in yourself and make sure that you go after the big ambition by means of which many years from now when you are hopefully in the same room with your children graduating you can look at them and be very proud that you were always

Risked it Vs regretting it.

WHAT YOU HAVE LEARNT NOW, MAKE SOME NOTES SO THAT YOU CANNOT FORGET

BOOKS RECOMMENDATION FROM RITESH

1) The hard thing about hard things

2) **Zero to One**

THE INTERNATIONAL BESTSELLER

ZERO TO ONE

NOTES ON STARTUPS,

OR

HOW TO BUILD THE FUTURE

PETER THIEL
WITH BLAKE MASTERS

'That rare thing: a concise, thought-provoking book on entrepreneurship' **THE TIMES**

3) **Biography of Elon Musk**

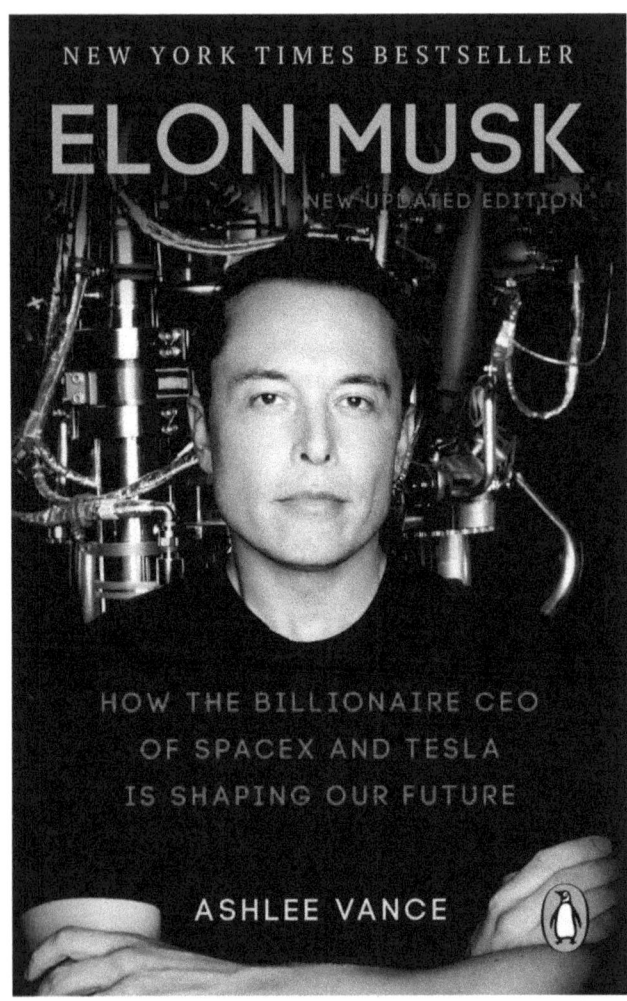

4) **Madhu Babu The Global Indian**

5) **NO Rules Rules**

NO RULES RULES
NETFLIX
and the
Culture of
Reinvention
REED
HASTINGS
ERIN
MEYER

RITESH'S ADVICE FOR YOUNG ENTREPRENEURS

For aspiring entrepreneurs out there who are scared of rejection - take pride in whatever you build. Don't fret about being rejected. All entrepreneurs get rejected at a point in their journey. The ones who take it in their stride succeed in the long run. Be Perseverant Always remember there is some light at the end of the tunnel and Have a lot of fun in the journey.

www.ingramcontent.com/pod-product-compliance
Lightning Source LLC
LaVergne TN
LVHW061540070526
838199LV00077B/6847